THE HERB-MOON

A FANTASIA

BY

John Oliver Hobbes

AUTHOR OF

SOME EMOTIONS AND A MORAL
A STUDY IN TEMPTATIONS
THE SINNER'S COMEDY
A BUNDLE OF LIFE

New York
International Association of Newspapers and Authors
1901

CONTENTS.

THE HERB-MOON

A Fantasia.

⚜

CHAPTER I.

Which Explains a Situation.

MISS CRECY, the rich brewer's only daughter, threatened to walk if her ponies did not trot faster.

"Whip the little creatures," she told her coachman, "but do not hurt them!"

They ambled through long winding roads hedged with white-thorn and black-thorn; past wheat-fields, bean-fields, fields of barley; past wide stretches of meadow enameled with buttercups and clover; past farmyards and little houses facing lawns; past inns and churches and the cemetery where *sheep's-parsley*—with

its long green stems and white delicate
flowers—waved over the graves, almost
as high as the headstones. There were
windmills and many small cottages to be
seen either near or in the distance; and
lanes, marked out by tall poplars or
young elms, ash and maple. Overhead
the sun shone out with a sleepy brilliance,
and gray clouds, like a swarm of fantastic pigeons, roamed, driven by the breeze,
across the sky.

As the phaeton turned a sudden corner,
Miss Crecy saw, some few yards ahead, a
young man, walking. He was tall, with
fine square shoulders and a resolute face.

"Can I give you a lift, Mr. Robsart?"
said the lady, when she reached him.

"Thanks," he replied, and stepped in
beside her.

Robsart was a clerk in a cotton factory,
and hoped, in time, to occupy the post of
overseer, formerly held by his father, now
dead. The situation demanded good

sense, patience, honesty, and every long
virtue; it belonged to that graceless order
of responsibilities where the least mistake
causes immense confusion, and the most
scrupulous attention is accepted as a matter of course. Neither enthusiasm nor
vanity had the smallest play in Robsart's
life: it was all a question of duty and conscience and self-respect. Sometimes he
resented its dullness and read about kings.
His own history, however, had not been
uneventful. At the time of his birth, his
father was senior partner in the honorable
firm—first established in 1700—of Robsart & Son, cotton spinners. The lad was
educated in the belief that he would, if
he lived, inherit the business and advance
a step further than his ancestors by repre-
senting his native town in the House of
Commons. He was sent to Eton, and
proceeded to Cambridge, where, at the end
of his first year, he was summoned to
Ottley, to find his father a bankrupt,

their home under the hammer, and the
factory sold to a Mr. Saxe, of Notting-
ham. It was a deadening blow. Old
Robsart was an easy-tempered body,
who, so long as he had a horse, good wine
and the best tobacco, asked little of any
one. He had married the daughter of
a famous Methodist, and having killed
her—not by cruelty but by his want of
religion (she had endeavored to make him
a Christian, and perished from the humiliation of her defeat)—he took for his
second wife a widow with a pinched
waist and easy morals, who, because she
did not dye her hair, was called no harder
name than injudicious for scattering
money as if it were sawdust and drinking
champagne by the pint. Robsart the
son was always courteous to this lady—
with Cromwell, " *he liked not war on
women* "—but he chafed in secret to think
that such a being could please the man
his mother had loved and prayed for.

The disgrace of the bankruptcy tried his proud spirit so far that he could only live by reminding himself that he might in time and by working pay every creditor to the full and restore the family's injured integrity. The older Robsart, with that distressing meekness which fills up the loss of self-respect, accepted the position of a salaried servant in the factory established by his forefathers. All forced virtue is degrading in its effect. Robsart senior withered away in his attempt to act divine characteristics with a heart convulsed by every human instinct of jealousy and resentment. His native good-humor failed him after the novelty of a subordinate post became merged in mere routine. To be reprimanded for un-punctuality—(he liked to rise at noon), to make way for Mr. Saxe, to be forbidden his cigar during office hours—these were the restrictions which stopped his breath. He could meet his unpaid butcher, but

he could not go out to luncheon at the
sound of the yard bell. He died in a
twelvemonth. His wife did not long sur-
vive him. She became annoyed with her
dressmaker, who used an inferior silk for
the lining of her funeral robes. A petty
law-suit ensued, and the little legacy left
her by her husband was just sufficient to
pay the costs of that litigation and her
burial fees. This sordid, unbeautiful finish to the hopes of Robsart's boyhood,
made a sad beginning for the second
epoch in his career. A less courageous
nature would have fled from the scene of
disappointment—seeking forgetfulness
in new surroundings, and a reputation
where his father was unknown. But he
chose instead to remain at Ottley. At
first, he was looked upon with a certain
mistrust, but before a year had passed,
he was treated as a gentleman by the
gentry and as a scholar by the poor.
His sad expression made him popular

with women, and his poverty saved him
from the envy of less handsome rivals.
Too poor to mix with the young men of
his own education, and too refined to asso-
ciate on any terms of intimacy with his
inferiors, too proud to accept hospitalities
he could not return, and too ambitious to
be easily resigned to a life of obscurity
and loneliness, his existence was often a
burden to himself and always an enigma
to his friends.

Miss Crecy, as she surveyed him slyly,
spoke, in maternal accents, of his pallor,
his evident ill-health. He was growing
thin; he needed a change; would he be
at the cricket-match to-morrow? Was he
not glad that croquet was coming into
fashion, and had he heard that Mr. Pope-
lard was engaged? No one had seen his
intended, but his mother looked greatly
relieved, so, no doubt, he was doing very
well for himself. Ottley was not a marrying place. The girls with money wanted

Army men, and the men with prospects
wanted to keep their liberty. For her
part, she put love before everything.
But perhaps she was sentimental.

By this time, the ponies had reached
the gates of a property known in the
neighborhood as Wentworth Place, formerly the homestead of the Robsarts, and
now the residence of Mr. Saxe, the cot-
ton-spinner.

"I am going to tea with Mrs. Saxe,"
exclaimed Miss Crecy. She would have
taken Robsart much further if he had but
promised to attend the cricket-match ;
as it was, she found him too ungrateful
a person for a young lady of her fortune
and amiability to waste time with.

" Good-bye," said she.

" Good-bye," said he.

His lodgings were at an old farmhouse
a mile or two beyond, and, as he turned
away from the chestnut avenue of Wentworth Place the home of his fathers for

six generations, the way before him looked steep and desolate. He had long passed that dramatic hour in grief when the very unexpectedness of the pang gives it at least the interest of a new experience. But now it had become a stale and voiceless sorrow—there was no more to be thought, or said, or done, and it was only when he felt a tightening of his heart that he knew that some sight or word had called the past once more to his remembrance.

They were felling the elm-trees which lined at grassy intervals the road; several great branches lay hewn upon the ground, and, here and there, a weeping willow or a small yew or a holly bush studded the turf. There was a horseless wagon in an enclosure beyond where a boy with a scythe stood, eating bread and butter, by a grindstone. He dropped the scythe to touch his cap to Robsart.

The path to Wrestle's Farm ran

through a wide, flat meadow, where chickens were cooped, cattle fed, and the laborers' children played. Now a jackdaw, now a magpie, now a rook and now a crow winged through the air, and the incessant twittering of birds made the stillness noisy. The house—half surrounded by a moat which served as a duck-pond—was small and moss-grown, two stories high and with three windows only. One could step in at the front door and out at the back in five strides. Robsart's parlor, which he shared with the parish organist and the organist's sister, Mrs. Arden, was in the right wing—as far as possible from the cow-shed, the teeming hay-yard, and the half-filled stables. To-day, as he reached the threshold, a shower, which had been threatening for some hours, fell from the sky. He stood and watched its play, heard its sharp singing, before he went to the sitting-room. Rose Arden was there at needlework, and as Robsart entered she smiled, sighed, and chose a brighter thread. The room was meagrely furnished; the long, low window, with its dim panes, opened out on a sunburnt lawn, hemmed in on one side by a brick wall and at the end by a hedge. There was a star-shaped flower-bed in the centre, where a rose-tree and some scarlet geraniums grew. The rest was mostly cut into strips and squares for gooseberry and currant bushes, cabbages, beans, and potatoes. When days were hot and insects hummed and buzzed, birds piped and the breeze blew fresh, the outlook was, though narrow, rather gay; but now the flowers were not yet in bloom, it rained, and an overpowering smell of humid earth made the air oppressive. Sometimes a raindrop, heavier than the others, fell with a dull splash on the window-sill, sometimes a rook flew over the distant tree-tops, but there was

no other sound to be heard—no other
living thing to see. Perhaps Rose was
glad to have no distraction from her
work: the wonderful stitches on her silk
coverlet multiplied, and the summer of
life she had never known seemed to grow
from under her fingers on to the blank
material beneath them.

Rose's face was not fair: the features,
though refined, were too irregular to be
gracious, and although her brow and soft
brown eyes were beautiful, they showed
the marks of over-long fatigue. An expression of intense sorrow veiled the
pretty liveliness of her mien, and it was
only when she laughed—which was seldom unless Robsart happened to be
present—that one saw how well merriment became her. She seemed about
five-and-thirty, although she was, in fact,
fully seven years younger. Her skin had
that curious waxen pallor often found in
women who, while they live in the coun-

try, breathing pure air, lose their color
and fade from lack of amusement. Oh,
those long days in the country—days of
anxiety without distraction, of patient
waiting for letters—no matter from whom
—which never come, days of trivial necessary tasks impossible to shirk yet so
wearisome in their accomplishment, days
when life can promise neither love, nor
youth, nor joy, nor even death—when
the world seems but a mighty grind-mill
where slaves eternally toil without rest
and without hire. The merest half-be-
lief in a living God will sustain many
souls through adversities and trials of
any picturesque or stirring order, but
only the most exalted faith can give one
the strength to bear in patience the
misery of loneliness, the constant fret of
uncongenial surroundings, the heavy burden of little common woes, which, because they are little and common, are so
humiliating. Rose had been born with

a spirit of adventure, which her uneventful life left undeveloped, and her frail body utterly belied. The story of her youth caused pity even in Ottley, where human sympathies ran in no rapid stream. Her husband, a lieutenant in the Navy, had lost his reason from the effects of a sunstroke, and was now in a private asylum. Rose was nineteen at the time of her marriage, and before her twentieth birthday she found herself in the terrible position of a young wife with no one to protect her, with no right to accept affection, with no right to bestow it, and with a craving for companionship so compelling, that in stifling it she broke her heart. When her only brother left Oxford, she went with him to the little town of Ottley, where he had accepted the post of parish organist, hoping, in time, to become choir-master at the cathedral. He was known to the Bishop as a young man of good character,

exceptional talents and most respectable
family : it was on his lordship's recom-
mendation that he was offered the situation he now occupied. That Rose should
live with her brother was considered
quite the best thing, and that Robsart
should form a third in the household
was not, on the whole, to be wondered
at. He was a steady, high-minded young
man, said current opinion, and had but
to see Mrs. Arden to understand the re-
lationship perfectly. She was a good
creature of any age, with no sort of fascination. It was all charming and platonic and idyllic. But such a pity! such
a pity! For Robsart was a fine-looking
fellow. One could be sure that he had
thrown away a number of chances solely
on account of his friendship for Edward
Banish and Mrs. Arden.

Rose, that day, had been restless in
Robsart's absence. She had been for a
little walk in the meadow, and changed

her dress twice. It struck her that she was growing old, and her gray alpaca gown of the summer before seemed, when she looked in the glass, a trying color. And she wept. It was not her custom to brood upon the past, yet this afternoon many things which she had long ceased to think of fell upon her mind. Several moments in her history came again with a pathos more vivid than her actual living of them. One had been —ah, many years back, in the small Catholic chapel of a little fishing-town in the south of England. It was an Easter Sunday, and she had wandered in to hear the Mass sung. Her seat faced the high altar, and when she gazed upon the cross it seemed, not an emblem of sorrow, but the mysterious key to the city of eternal happiness. There were lilies below and around ; flame-colored azaleas and deep-purple flowers of some homelier variety ; the gold on the priest's vestments shone

in the candle-light, and, through one
stained-glass window, a ray of the sun lit
up a wooden figure of the Virgin, curi-
ously carved, with onyx eyes and a robe
of some glittering stuff embroidered by
nuns. Rose observed all these things
just as one scans the features of a well-
known face or a familiar spot: if there
had been no visible flowers, no sun, no
candles, or no gold, their meaning, nevertheless, would still have seemed there—
like the true elements in a fantastic
dream. The Great Sacrifice was made;
the celebrant, the deacons and the acolytes
filed out to joyous music and in solemn
procession: one by one each worshiper
left the building: Rose was alone. For
that celestial minute, she felt that despair
and sin and grief and disappointment had
passed away for ever, that the peace of
God, making all things perfect, was come
upon the land—never to depart again
therefrom. She prayed without words:

her spirit sang its song of thanksgiving in
silence; life was so sweet; eternity, so
brief; heaven, so like a fairer earth. She
thought of the saints and martyrs till her
heart thrilled with passionate admiration
and a fearful longing for the power to
suffer, endure, and conquer similarly.
Ah, if one could but be sure of that ulti-
mate triumph! There was the doubt—
the burden. What of the souls who
fought, yet apparently failed—dying, unknown, unacknowledged, all their labors
unrewarded; who turned aside from the
broad way, yet, for some reason, were
not to be found upon the narrow one?
The saints who had no day! Had any
one sung their histories, preached their
martyrdom? Her impetuous spirit
paused at a plan of life which, in her judgment, made the pleasures of this world
insipid, yet left the recompense of the
white future undefined. She was young,
ardent—full of hope and splendid vigor;

she longed for combats, temptations, trials of faith, hardship, persecution—longed for them because she felt so sure that nothing could dismay her; nothing overcome her pride of girlhood. Most of us in our apprentice days feel mighty enough to bear the burden of success, but how many have the strength to fail? How many would dare to choose the gift of failure? The question pursued her; it carried the accent of defiance. Yet, she thought, why not forget the crowning victory or the final humiliation, whichever it might be: the task was the thing —the task—a faithful answer to one's calling. And her calling was not to high places or through dazzling paths; she was going to be married and live very humbly. . . . Oh, how long ago it was! She was a girl then, and she used to laugh all day. How long ago it was! Arden had been a bad husband; he was often drunk and he did not know how to treat

a refined woman. Yet she had cared for
him because he loved her after his own
brutal fashion : in the intervals of churl-
ishness and ill-temper, he would read
poetry alóud and kiss her pretty hands,
take her to the theatre, or buy flowers.
Then, after eight strange months, came
the sunstroke and all the horror of insan-
ity. She had tried to keep him at home,
but he killed their dog, and would have
killed her too : so they took him away.
He could never recover, they said. She
cried for two years, and studied art
needlework. She could now earn enough
money to keep herself very comfortably
and pay for her brother's annual trip to
Switzerland. He was delicate. Robsart
came into her existence, she knew not
how. He was her brother's friend, and he
was living at Ottley when they first came
there : they had agreed to settle altogether at the farmhouse. That was all.
But in the woman's mind the story turned

upon one scene which happened when they had been in Ottley just three months. Edward had gone to the choir practice, and she and Robsart were together, sitting idly, in the parlor. They talked about spring, and ideals, and the nightingale.

"You know," said Robsart, quite suddenly, "that I love you."

"Yes," she answered.

They looked into the night of each other's eyes till day seemed to dawn in them.

"There is nothing to fear," said he, "in love—in affection."

She glanced past him, out on to the world she had, for too long a second, forgotten. The curtains had not been drawn, and she could see the barren garden where darkness seemed to flow like a silent tide—flooding the land with mystery. Alone it swept—the greatest, most solitary of all lonelinesses. Robsart followed the direction of her gaze, and with something like jealousy, drew down the frayed, green blinds.

"There is nothing to see," he said, "there is no moon."

She leaned her head against the shutter and trembled into tears.

"Don't cry," said Robsart. "Oh, Rose, do not cry!"

"I am not—I am not," she whispered, and sobbing, stole past him out of the room.

For weeks she had been happy enough in the knowledge that he was near her: she had been a listener for his footsteps— for the sound of his voice. And now she knew what this meant. It was all wrong. They could never again watch the sky together or listen to the nightingale or wander through the fields at sunset; they could never again smile at lovers when they met them, Sunday evenings, on the road from church. Robsart seemed to understand that these things were at an end, and once, when he surprised her in tears, he spoke quite roughly about the bad starch they used for his collars.

"Perhaps the fault is in the ironing," she suggested.

"I shall make a row about it," said he, and, as he dared not look longer at her poor, pale face, he went out, walked miles, and came home too tired to eat his supper.

As Rose sat at her eternal needlework, her throat would swell : she felt the exceeding bitter cry but could not utter it, and her lips grew more compressed, and the lines round her mouth more deep, and the fire in her temples more cruel. At two-and-twenty love does not leave us laughing.

"I must go to Lauderston," said Robsart, one day; "this place does not agree with me."

This was more than she could bear.

"Wait another month," she pleaded, "till the pear-trees are in bloom. They look so pretty!"

So he stayed, and every week he found it easier to remain. Rose became so dull. By degrees and after many cruel shocks to his sentiment, he began to own to himself her poverty of personal attractions, and he thought he must have seen her before under the glamour of a foolish, incomprehensible passion. She watched his love die out: she killed the lover in him just as she had slain the woman in herself. She told her heart, which was too numb to ache, that it was better so. She ceased to care very much for his company; but then she no longer cared for anything: she felt chilled by her own coldness. She still said her prayers—the Our Father and a quaint little hymn she had been taught when a child, but she made no special petitions—named no

names. It may be that she dared not.
Yet she never called herself unhappy, for
she had so many orders for her needlework. She read Thomas à Kempis and
tried to follow the " Imitation of Christ."
Of course, she fell behind often, and often
wondered whether a rule so hard could
ever be entirely obeyed. Other rules,
however, which read more sweetly seemed
to lead to mistakes and griefs yet darker ;
so, obedient and uncomplaining, she
struggled on in the old groove. Her
time—that second unmarked time one
has apart from one's daily occupation—
was spent in waiting on the two men
whose sitting-room she shared. She
studied their tastes, lived in their work,
bore with their moods and humors.
Edward suffered heroic pains from some
internal malady. Days when he felt
bright he would be wildly boisterous : he
would shout, sing, play the fool, and,
after an hour of undisciplined hilarity,

become quarrelsome. At other times he had only dark looks, ominous mutterings, and no appetite. When these fits were upon him, poor Rose used to shed dry tears in her lonely corner—fearing some calamity, she knew not what. In the evenings, two of the three would play chess, or one would read aloud while the others listened, or they would go for a walk, or they would each take a book. On rare occasions they went to enter-tainments at the Town Hall, but they had always to leave early on account of Edward's health, or because the music was too outrageous for his scholarly ear. Rose rather liked songs with a valse refrain, and once she greatly enjoyed a wretched performance of *My Wife's Second Floor*. Edward, in consequence, would hardly speak to her for a week. He was a man of violent prejudices. Yet when Rose tried to resent his tyran-nical conduct, the remembrance of his

many acts of kindness, his noblesse, his
tenderness caught her soul, stealing over
her desolation like the morning sunshine
over bleak hills.　He was editing an
edition of Bach, correcting, suggesting,
annotating, but all that was as nothing :
he longed to give voice to the symphonies
in his own brain, and because he could
not, he suffered, like some wretch in
chains—tongue-tied, yet with a golden
message to tell could he but utter it.
His worse moods were those of religious
melancholy, which afflicted him to madness.　He had composed a few chorales
under this influence, but Rose shuddered
when she heard them, and found no
beauty in harmonies born of such dis-
sonant emotions.

Sometimes Robsart would discover
that she looked ill, and they would
arrange to take her for a drive in the
trap.　It took half an hour to harness the
pony ; Susan (who managed the farm)

held the cart, and Adam, her husband,
fumbled with the reins; Robsart and
Edward, looking on, would add confusion
to the scene by interference. Then a
discussion would follow: who should
drive? And which way should they go?
Rose's suggestions were seldom if ever
regarded, and the weary woman would
usually find herself being shaken over the
bleakest part of the country with Edward,
moaning over his liver, at her back, and
Robsart, wondering how soon they could
get home, by her side. Both men were
devoted to her: neither of them had ever
seen a woman whom he thought her equal,
but they never had time to tell her so
and were, in any case, too shy to even let
her guess it. Love, however, is a state
of giving—and unconscious giving—and
Rose never looked for praise or gratitude.
When they carried her off on these unprof-
itable excursions, she saw the kindly
motive under their apparent savagery and

even found the exquisite pleasure they
sought to give her, in suffering so much
for the satisfaction of their conscience.
Once on returning from an exceptionally
painful encounter with the east wind
over sharp stones, she heard Robsart
encouraging poor Edward by a reminder
—"that after all, Rose enjoyed a drive
and it did her so much good!"

She learned to speak not of herself. In
their sitting-room the boards groaned, the
wind moaned, the flies droned, but Rose
was nearly always silent. She talked
when her advice was invited, and Edward
had often been pleased to call her "no
fool"; she considered all subjects in their
relation to Robsart and her brother: in
every discussion she counted herself—her
own desires, her own heart, her own
hopes—as nothing in the world. She
dreaded giving counsels of perfection and
was often, in her conversation, so liberal-
minded as to astonish Robsart, who found

such worldly-wisdom—while he acted on
it—by no means charming in a woman.
When he entered the room after his drive
with Miss Crecy, some of the old amazement—even disbelief—fell upon him that
he had ever been desperately, deeply, sor-
rowfully in love with the plain and aging
woman who sat there, gray in the face,
embroidering doves and butterflies on a
pink silk quilt.   And as she worked, she
sang—

> O weep, my heart, for Summer days are fled,
> The earth is cold, and roses that were red,
> Birds that once sang, and little things that flew
> Are dead.
>
> The pallid day is moist with chilling dew,
> There is no noon, because the wind that blew
> The clouds across the sun, is stern, poor heart,
> Like you.

"Dear God!" he said, when she had
finished.   "Sing something cheerful."

Rose smiled, and he noticed the grave

of a dimple in her cheek. Presently he
mentioned that Chloe Crecy had met him
on the high-road and given him a lift in
her pony carriage.

"She's a nice girl," said Rose; "good-
natured! kind!"

"She bores me," he answered.

"I am sorry," said Rose. She grew
white and made a clumsy stitch.

"Do you ever think of marrying?"
said she.

"What do you mean?"

"Do you ever think of marrying?" she
repeated.

"I believe," she went on, "you have
been with us so long that you think—it
would be unkind to leave us."

"Oh no!" said Robsart, "men are not
like that."

He had never considered the question,
but instinct gave him its answer. He
stayed with Edward and Rose because he
liked their society. That much, at least,

was clear in his mind—marriage or no marriage.

"Men are not like that," he said, again.

Then he went out into the garden and sat under the old plum-tree and stared at a little white gate which led to the paddock. He forgot the rain, although it was falling fast.

CHAPTER II.

Philosophy and Vegetables.

IT was Susan who called him in.

"La, sir!" said she, "what are you thinking of? Do you want to catch your death? Your coat is sopping wet? If Mrs. Arden should see you! But there! you are worse than a child. Really, sir, you'd worry any one's life out."

He went into the bright small kitchen where she was chopping onions, and he warmed himself at the fire.

"Is it cold to-day?" he asked.

"Cold?" said Susan; "it's enough to roast you! You've caught a chill as sure as Fate."

"As sure as Fate," said Robsart. "I like that!"

The woman looked at him sharply and nodded her head.

"There's nothing like dandelion at this time of the year," said she; "it's beautiful. I'd give something if the black sow would take it, but she's too crafty. She enjoys herself, she do, when she's in a temper. And there's no living in the same field with her. Adam has put her all alone in the cuckoo-flower meadow, and she lords about it like a duchess! And it's all because she got a prize at the Fair. A nicer sow I never had till she got that prize. And do what we will, we can't suit her. She won't look at Speckly—who pleased her well enough last year. I don't hold with giving prizes. But I'm waiting till she gets lonely. She wants to be admired—that's all. When she looks about the meadow and finds nothing but cuckoo-flowers, she'll be civil enough to Speckly. Trust her! And if I could afford to let him have his self-respect, he shouldn't go

nigh her. A proud trollop! Oh! I *shall*
be pleased when I see her getting lonely."

"I observe," said Robsart, "that you
believe in the sobering quality of afflic-
tion."

"Aye! that I do. Do you think I
should have married if I hadn't been
lonely? Not I. But I shouldn't have
married so soon if I had seen London
first. I do like it—but it is unsettling.
Last May I went up for three days and I
spent eight pound. I went everywhere
and I paid for everybody! And why
not? we have no children. Adam is
nothing for life—what I call *life*—knowing what's going on and all that. He says
he can't see anything in it. He's so quiet
and he wouldn't dress properly. I don't
mind how he goes about on the farm—
but in London! Do you think he would
put on a white shirt and look gentleman-
like? Not he. He doesn't so much
mind a blue *and* white shirt, but an all

white—never.   He says he's only a laboring man and doesn't want to be taken for
his betters.   He's an excellent husband
is Adam, but he's dull.   I like life," she
repeated.   " I sha'n't stop here for ever.
When I make up my mind to go, I shall
go.   If I waited for Adam to give the
word, I should never get anywhere.   But
wherever I go, he'll follow me fast enough.
That's one comfort."

" I suppose you wouldn't like it, if he
did not follow you ? " said Robsart.

Susan tossed her head.

" Lor'!" she answered, " he knows
when he's well off.   He's wiser than many
that can talk the hind-legs off a donkey
and look a lot.   There's that girl Ethel as
thinks of marrying young Bates.   ' Shall
I marry him ? ' says she to me.   ' I can
tell you nothing,' says I, ' but marry a
man with a head on his shoulders !   Marry
a man with a head on his shoulders, that's
what I say.'   And that's all she got out

of me. I was scrooping up onions just
as I am scrooping 'em now. Mrs. Arden
was sitting where you are sitting. She
often comes in to get cheered up."

"And what did she say?"

"Nothing, because I gave Ethel a look.
It isn't kind to talk about sweethearts before Mrs. Arden—when she can't have
one. It's really enough to make anybody un-Christian to see a nice lady like
that sewing all day long with no one to
think of and nothing to look forward to.
Is it natural? And I don't call her so
plain, myself. Her eyes are almost as
big as the Queen of Beauty's in that al-
manac over your head, and her figure is
as nice a figure as I ever saw. Doctor
Somers was here the other afternoon about
Adam's chest, and Mrs. Arden happened
to pass the window. 'She must have
been a very pretty girl,' said he, 'and it's
my belief that she makes herself look old
on purpose.' And if he ever spoke a

true word it was that, for I have been in her room of a morning and caught her with her hair down her back and her neck and arms bare, and I hardly knew her. I would have said that she wasn't a day more than six-and-twenty—and we all know that if a woman is old, she shows it plain enough if you see her before she's up and had her breakfast. I could shed every tear in my body when I think of Mrs. Arden, and I wish that old husband of hers would break his neck. The Lord forgive me for saying so! As I have never seen her husband—and don't want —there is no harm done in wishing he was dead! And there's your coat steaming like a wet blanket, and you pay no more heed to it than if there was no such thing as rheumatics. Here! give it to me."

He took off his coat and handed it to Susan without a word.

"Lor'!" she exclaimed, with a giggle,

"the onions have got into your eyes. They *do* look bad."

She watched him go up the creaking staircase to his bedroom.

"He's upset," she said to herself. "Those was the gentlest onions I ever chopped. It wasn't them."

CHAPTER III.

What the Herb-Moon Means.

THE good creature went out to milk
the cows, but all the time she grieved
about Robsart and wondered why he
looked so sad. At last she found a reason for his melancholy, and she longed
so much to tell some one of her belief, that,
as Adam had gone to the brewery to complain of the last cask of ale, and it was
impossible to remain silent till his return,
she sought Mrs. Arden. Rose was still
sitting at the window with her needlework. She had made three butterflies
with golden and amethyst wings while
Robsart had been thinking under the
plum-tree and talking in the kitchen.

" Is that you, Susan?" said she.

"Yes," said Susan, who had now a pain in her throat from running or some other cause. "I have got one of my worrying fits, I have. I've heard something and I don't know whether I ought to tell it. It's no affair of mine and yet it is. I can't bear injustice, and if any one expects me to look on and see injustice, they don't know Susan! They are not doing the right thing by Mr. Robsart at the factory. And he's too proud to complain. It's just like him to let himself be put upon."

Rose stuck her needle into her needle-book and sat back a little further in the shade.

"It was Doctor Somers who told me," continued Susan. "There's changes to be made at the factory, and Mr. Robsart should now, by rights, be manager. And they say that long-nosed Grayson will get the situation because he's a married man with twins. Of course, it stands to

reason that a married man is more of a
man than an unmarried: married men,
too, are supposed to be steadier, they
have more mouths to feed and more to
put up with—in one way or another.
And it's a woman's place to take the part
of husbands and show a feeling heart for
them—it's foolhardiness and nothing else
to trapse about from house to house going on against marriage. But fair's fair,
and Grayson has only been in the factory a twelvemonth : while Mr. Robsart
knows the business through and through.
I say myself he ought to think of settling
—for what sort of life is it with no wife
and no proper home? I should be the
loser if he left me and set up for himself,
but I can't help seeing that it would be
all for his own good."

Poor Rose could not speak, but, pre-
tending to search for a pin, she held her
hand to her heart.

"Tommy was in here just now," added

Susan, "and his eyes are all over the place. He saw Miss Crecy get as red as a beet when she met Mr. Robsart on the road this afternoon. She gave him a lift in her new pony-shay as far as Ottley Dene, and her groom gave Tommy a wink a yard long when he saw the performance. Miss Crecy will have a nice bit of money one of these days, and ' Randalls ' is a pleasant-standing house."

"Yes," said Rose, "a very pleasant-standing house. I remember the orchard."

"And Mr. Robsart is so fond of apples!" said Susan. "When he marries, I hope it will be straight off without shilly-shally. For there's nothing so wearing as the herb-moon."

"The herb-moon?" repeated Rose, stupefied.

"Aye! That's my name for one of these long courtships. Adam and I did all our courting in a fortnight: that's why we are happy. This walking out with each other year in and year out, till all your nerve is gone and you are sick with talking, was never to my taste nor to my mother's before me. 'Tisn't natural, and I'm all for nature, I am."

At that moment, Edward, with a roll of music under his arm, came into the room; and Susan, who was always afraid of the organist because he liked to walk alone in the moonlight, hurried away.

Rose took up her coverlet, and told her brother, while she stitched, Susan's news about the changes at the factory.

"I hate gossip," said Edward, who had a shaggy beard and big eyebrows.

"But this affects Robsart," answered Rose. "I think you ought to tell him that the factory people are right. He should get married."

"He can't get married to order," said Edward. "Marriage is a thing which has to come into your mind. Women, I know, think of nothing else. But men are different. I wish you wouldn't distract me with all this petty tittle-tattle when I want to work. I had an idea for my opera, and now it has gone."

As Edward's ideas for his masterpiece were always of so frail a nature that even a coal dropping into the grate could make him forget them, Rose did not reproach herself bitterly for venturing to address him yet further.

"You don't understand me," she said. "I think it is your duty to have a serious talk with Louis. He has lived with us now for three years, and as he knows you dislike any change in your life, it is clearly right that you should make it easy for him to leave us. He is so kind that he would suffer many disadvantages rather than give any one the least pain. I am sure I value his company quite as much as you do, but we must not be selfish."

" No doubt," said Edward, " you find it quite a light matter to renounce my friends and my pleasures ! To say that you value Robsart's company is a mere phrase, since you are never, by any chance, with him for any longer time than you can help—that is, at meals and at church. So far as I can gather you have not one taste in common, and, if he had not a singularly good disposition, he would never stand your indifference. But I should find my life insupportable without him : he is the only man with the least intelligence in the parish, and, as he has a very fair knowledge of music, he is the one person who can drill the choir or take my place when I am ill. I could get an assistant, no doubt ; but a professional would be longing for my death in order that he might step into my shoes, or else he would try to show at every opportunity how much better he played than I. Robsart is always modest, and never once thinks that because he is an excellent amateur who has learned a great deal in spare moments, he can instruct those who have given up their whole life and youth to the study of one art. Yet you tell me I ought to urge him to go away from us and marry! All women are full of ca- prices, and I never pretended to under- stand them. I used to think that you had more good sense than the rest—partly because of your troubles, and partly because you are generally too hard at work to waste time running to and fro tale-bearing, scandal-mongering, and match-making like the others. But in this instance you have shown yourself extremely weak and a person of no judg- ment. I hope you will never again en- courage Susan to give you her vulgar— though possibly well-meant—advice : you are not strong enough to resist the com- monplace! I can see now that nothing would give you greater happiness than to

ruin poor Robsart's individuality by plant-
ing him in an Ivy Lodge with a wife and
six children!"

Rose smiled very sadly, and replied
with much sweetness:

"I am sorry that I appear to you so
foolish. The prospect of seeing Louis in
an Ivy Lodge does not, however, delight
me so much as you suppose! But I have
too much faith in his heart and his character to fear that the responsibility of
either a wife or even six children would
destroy his courage for ever and spoil his
career! In any case, his actual marriage
is not our business. Indeed, I am so
fond of him—although you may not believe it—that while I could trust my
reasons for urging him to marry, I could
not trust those I might see against such
a step. I should suspect them of selfishness. Our duty is to leave him free to
take a wife if he felt so minded. It is
always said that while a man has a fairly

comfortable home he will not trouble himself to look out for another. Of course, our rooms are not at all luxurious, but they are tidy; and Susan can cook as well as any servant in the district. I know that I myself would not be missed very much from the household, yet every woman counts where a man's home-life is concerned. I mend Louis's things, and dust his books, and keep order."

"Men are not so weak as you think," said Edward. "They can always leave anybody or any place without a pang—if they find another person or another place they like better. If they feel pricks and scruples it is merely because they cannot make up their mind that the change will be absolutely to their advantage. I am your brother and I do not lie to you. Other men would perhaps encourage your delusions. The moment Robsart is not happy with us, he will pack up his box and go. He will find it quite easy."

"But," said Rose, in a low voice, "perhaps he ought not to be happy with us. We are bad friends, thinking only of ourselves, if we encourage him to remain here against his own interests."

She believed that she understood Robsart far better than her brother, who judged every one by his own measure. But Rose also judged every one by her own measure. She would have thought it extremely difficult to leave any friends who seemed to depend on her society for their peace of mind and with whom she had been living for three years. And of course there was another consideration too, which Edward could not take into the reckoning because he knew nothing about it. That was Robsart's former love for herself. He still liked her a little, though not so much, perhaps, but he could forget her if she went away. Yet how could she explain this?

"Has it ever occurred to you," she

said at last, "that Louis felt a certain—
pity—for me?"

"What do you want with his pity
when I am alive to look after you?"
growled Edward.

Rose forced back her tears and spoke
no more, till, several minutes later, she
heard Robsart's voice in the passage.

" Here he is," she said, and, picking up
her work-basket, left the room just as he
entered it.

When she had gone, Edward gave a
great sigh, and struck his head with his
palms.

"What is the matter with Rose?" he
asked. "She has never been so tiresome."

"It must be the thunder in the air,"
said Robsart. "I feel rather cross myself."

"But she isn't cross," said Edward;
"she is only worrying about things which
don't concern her."

The two men looked at each other, and
heard her light footsteps in the room
overheard.

"Young Hartopp told me that you
were driving with Chloe Crecy," said the
organist, who, perhaps because he was
rather weakly and ill and therefore dependent on his friends, was always unrea-
sonably jealous of them. "I observe,"
he went on, "that the love-making we
find in the world is mostly mere vanity.
A woman is not so grateful for affection
as she is anxious to show others how
much some one is devoted to her, and a
great many men are equally self-seeking.
It is all show and parade and pirouetting.
It never took me in. I have not spoken
two words to Chloe Crecy in my life, but
I'm sure she's a minx."

"Oh, she's a nice creature—good-
natured! kind!" said Robsart, who, having no decided opinion of his own with
regard to Miss Crecy, thought he could
not do better than quote Rose.

"Ah!" said Edward, "you will be marrying one of these days. I see it all."

But Robsart was wondering why Rose had started from the room the very moment that he appeared on the threshold.

"And what is all this about Grayson being made manager?" continued Edward.

Robsart lit his pipe and reflected for a few seconds.

"Grayson is manager at this moment," he answered, at last; "the place was filled up yesterday."

"Well," said Edward, indignantly, "you might have told us. It isn't pleasant to learn that every passer-by knows more about your friends than you do yourself."

"There was nothing to tell," said Robsart; "how could I suppose that you took any interest in Grayson?"

"I take a considerable interest in him when I see him placed over your head! If you are going to endure treatment of that sort you are a coward and I quite agree with Rose."

" I am sorry Rose thinks me a coward."

"Any sensible woman would say the same. Why have they given Grayson the preference?"

" He is a married man. He has far more need of the extra salary than I have. You must admit that a sane reason."

"You can't be serious," said Edward, growing more angry. " Just as if you couldn't let yourself go in my presence, at any rate, and call it—what you must think it—a parcel of cant and twaddle. Here's a young ass, who, because he has married an old harridan for her money, is thought more trustworthy than you are! I will never believe it: there must be something else behind it all. The British nation has not won its flag by teaching doctrines of rancidity! We are a mercenary lot and a snobbish lot, but I swear that we are not fools."

Robsart smiled.

" To be quite candid, then," said he, " I

haven't told you all. They are going to move the manager's office to Lauderston —they are starting new works there. And I—I didn't care to go away from Ottley. Lauderston is too dirty and too crowded and too noisy: I prefer the country."

"Then they offered you the manager-ship?"

"Yes, but I don't wish it known."

"Every one will think that you have been passed over."

"That doesn't matter in the least."

Edward was too bewildered—too agitated to speak. Lauderston was thirty miles away. How could he urge his friend to go to Lauderston? Yet how could he wish him to remain when remaining meant the forfeiture of four hundred a year, a house, and even better prospects? The poor invalid suffered agonies between the selfishness he had acquired through many wants and the generosity he had been

born with. Then he remembered, that,
fortunately, the decision had been already
made. Had not Robsart taken the whole
burden of the refusal on his own shoulders? Edward never suspected that the
younger man had foreseen this struggle
and mercifully spared him its bitterness
as well as its responsibility.

" But I should like them all to know,"
said he, " that you declined the place.
You are in a false position otherwise."

" It must never be mentioned," replied
Robsart, rather sternly. " I ask you to
respect my wish. I shall tell Rose because—as you say she is annoyed about
the gossip—it would be unfair to let her
misunderstand the true facts. What
other people think or hint or imagine is
of no consequence."

Then Susan came in bearing the supper-
tray and made Edward's head ache by
letting the bread-platter fall, loaf and all,
on the floor, with a crash.

CHAPTER IV.

Which Shows that Lovers can at Times Talk Reason.

AFTER supper, the organist went, for it was Tuesday, to the choir-practice. To his great surprise and disappointment, Robsart did not, as usual, offer to accompany him. Rose began to tremble just as she had trembled on just such an evening three years before. She looked very pale and very tired: there were heavy lines under her eyes and she could scarcely hold up her head.

"It is a long while," began Robsart. "since we have had a talk. I don't know that I have very much to say now. But first I must tell you about Grayson."

He explained the matter as briefly as

possible and watched her face as he had
not watched it for many months. " Why
isn't she pretty," he wondered, " when
everything about her is pretty? If she
had more color, and unbraided her hair
and rested her eyes and wore brighter
gowns, she would be charming. Yet I
hate red cheeks, and as for her hair—
what can be neater than braids? No
amount of fatigue can alter the shape of
her eyes, and when she is so tidy and has
such a graceful figure—why should she
deck herself in finery? I see nothing
wrong in her, for, on the contrary, if she
were in any respect different, she would
not be half so sweet." He was, however,
unable to study her so carefully as he
could have wished because she was not
sewing, and it is difficult to treat a woman
like a picture when she sits opposite you
and smiles from time to time.

" I think you were wrong," said Rose,
" not to go to Lauderston. A man

should be ambitious, and if God sends
you an opportunity to advance in the
world, you are not merely ungrateful but
cowardly if you do not take it. You say
that you prefer to live in the country:
that is a poor excuse for being indolent."

At this he was deeply hurt, and was
far too proud to make any reply. As
for Rose, she had such a pain in her heart
and such wild thoughts in her head that
she feared she would surely lose her wits.

"I hope it is not too late," she continued, " to tell them that you spoke too
hastily and have changed your mind."

" If it were not too late, I should never
see the matter in any other light. I do
nothing hastily, and I am a man of my
word. I know what I want and what I
do not want. I know what I can do and
what I cannot do. I could not go to
Lauderston."

Rose, for some reason, dared not ask
him why he felt such a dislike for a

town he had visited once or twice and had always, until this day, spoken well of.

"I knew I could not go there," he went on, "but I did not know why I could not till I thought it all out under the plum-tree. I want to stay with you. Although I may be nothing in your life, you are everything in mine, and so long as I do not offend you, or tire you, or hinder you, you have no right to send me away. I will not tell you that I love you, because such things cannot be said between us, and if they were said they would mean little. I am in no mood to make protestations, and you are not free to hear them. I don't ask for much of your company—it does not give me any special happiness to be with you. But I like to know that you are here— that if you were ill or in trouble, I could take care of you and protect you."

"I will not be your stumbling-block," said Rose, trying to speak like an old woman, and looking, Robsart thought, like an angel; "I am very fond of you, too, dear, and I am more grateful than I can ever explain for your friendship and your sympathy. Yet, while I value both, I do not need either so much as you think, for I have forgotten all my sorrow and I am quite happy. Youth is the time for love and grief, and I am no longer young. I forget my age, but as I am so contented and I find work so pleasant, I know I must be much older than most people! You are far too manly to spend your time protecting some one who stands in no need of protection and taking care of some one who is already provided for."

Robsart understood her nature too well to think her either cold or heartless for saying such things to him, so although he was perplexed, he loved her all the better and was more than ever persuaded that braids were the most admirable way

of dressing the hair—particularly when
the hair was auburn and looked as though
it were meant to dance and glisten.

"You are not my stumbling-block,"
said he; "and if there is any good in
me, I owe it all to you. I could not
have worked—if you had not encouraged
me by your patience: I should have
done all manner of foolish things—if I
had not always remembered that I would
have to see you the next day: I would
have been a false friend to Edward if
you had not kept me true. Do you
think I have forgotten that evening when
we stood over there by the window—and
I kissed you and you left me? Do you
think that made me love you less?"

His voice failed, and he bit his lip.
Rose longed to touch him, but she sat
quite still.

"Do you know what it is," he said, at
last, "to feel divided against yourself—
separate from yourself? Did you ever

feel sick, starved, bruised? That is the way I nearly always feel, and if I worked twelve hours a day and if I went to the ends of the earth, I should be just the same. But while you are with me, I am not quite so wretched."

Rose stood up and placed her chair back in its place against the wall.

"I want you to promise me," she said, "that you will go to Lauderston. It would not be fair to Grayson to take the managership now, but you can tell them that you will go in some other capacity. I ask this not for your sake, but for mine."

"For your sake?" he said; "for your sake? Do you want me to go?"

"Yes," she answered. "I think we must not meet again for a long, long time. This is all wrong and madness. We must not deceive each other or ourselves. I have been living a lie for three years and I am being punished for

it. I meant to be a good influence in
your life, and I find I have been an evil
one. I prided myself on being unselfish,
when I must have known that I was
thinking solely of my own happiness. I
could avoid you ; I could pretend not to
think of you ; I could flatter myself all
day that you were a friend and no more;
I could do everything—anything, all
things except leave you. I had the courage to see you like me less and less ; I had
the courage to weary you by my silence
and my plainness ; I had the courage to
bury myself alive, to fade, to wither, to
work, work—work—against time, against
my own despair, my own madness, but I
had not the courage to go away or to
ask you to go. And was it love which
made me so contemptible? I think not.
If you care for me, help me to be strong
—help me to be honest."

He hesitated.

"Why," she asked, "don't you wish

people to hear that you refused to go to Lauderston? Because you know they would say it was on my account. And they would be right, Louis! They would be right! Why are you ashamed to have them guess the reason? Because your conscience tells you that you are wrong."

"They would misjudge—they would never understand—"stammered Robsart.

"You are not a man to mind what the world said of you, if you felt that you were acting an honorable part. No one can be brave and defy others when he has lost his own self-respect. And I have brought this upon you—I—who meant to be your friend. I have taught you to be a hypocrite, to walk softly and fear opinion: I have wasted your will and your manhood."

"Rose! Rose! Rose!"

"I have tried to make myself indispensable to you. There may have been

frowns on my face, but you always found
flowers in your room. And you knew
who put them there. That has been my
method all through—it was all in under-
currents, and in hidden ways—never
frank, never in broad sunlight. Oh,
promise me that you will go!"

"You ask a hard thing."

"Promise me," she repeated. "It is
the only favor I have ever begged from
you."

Robsart had not accepted one word of
Rose's self-condemnation, for he knew
full well the woman she was, and neither
anything that others might say about
her, nor anything she might imagine
against herself could make him think
her other than the least selfish soul he
had ever met or heard of. She saw this
faith in his face, and although she had
meant him to think her, and indeed
thought herself, quite unworthy of such
trust, she could not help feeling glad

that she was dear to one whom, she was not afraid to own, she loved above any creature on earth.

"Promise me," she cried, once more, "that you will go."

"And what of Edward?" he asked.

Rose looked at him in despair.

"I had forgotten Edward," she said. "He would soon get tired of living alone with me. Oh, what shall I do?"

Robsart felt the blood grow warm once more in his veins, for the fear of leaving Rose had seemed to change him to stone.

"It would kill Edward to lose you," she murmured; "he cannot live without sympathy, and no one is so kind to him as you are."

"You see!" said Robsart; "I have acted for the best."

The poor woman smiled, and, going behind him, placed a hand on each of his shoulders, and looked down on him as though he were a child who had stumbled through a lesson with more pains than success.

"You acted generously," she whispered; "don't think I can ever forget it," then, as she could not add more because of the anguish of her soul, she went quickly away, blind with tears, to her own room.

CHAPTER V.

Susan Sheds Tears.

THE next morning, after Robsart had gone to the factory and while Edward was at church, practising, Rose told Susan that she would be leaving Ottley that day for London. As she went there twice a year or oftener on business connected with her needlework, Susan showed no surprise at the news.

"But," said Rose, "I do not wish my brother to know that I am going, because leave-takings make him very ill, and, as you remember, the scene last time I went away exhausted every one in the house! But if he comes home as usual and finds me absent, he will make the best of it at once and wait patiently till I return."

Here she checked herself, and stood where Susan could not see her face. She had been awake most of the night, saying things over and over again, and watching for daylight.

" Mr. Edward is just like a child," said Susan, as she knotted the cords of Mrs. Arden's box—which stood between the mahogany chest of drawers and the dressing-table draped with flowered muslin over pink calico ; " he will never be manly till he's married."

"You want to marry everybody," said Rose, laughing in spite of her grief.

"To be sure," said Susan, "for marriage is natural. Mr. Edward would have found a wife long ago if you hadn't taken such care of him—treating him like a pet lamb and talking to him as if he was an old maid. Never let a man forget that he's a man—that's what I say. It's mothers and sisters who make half the bad husbands you hear about—for no wife worth the name wants to keep her man short-coated! But if many women could have their will, they would make their boys and brothers wear christening robes and eat pap till they turned fifty— aye, and more. And it isn't love so much as wanting to have their own way with 'em and to have 'em like rabbits in a cage. Lord; I know by myself. I could keep Adam hanging on my arm all day if I hadn't the sense to see it would make him a softie. There's enough real children in the world for women to look after without dilly-dallying about with grown men. When I get one of these petting moods on, I just call on my poor sister—who is a widow with nine— and I just set to work mending their clothes and washing their heads—the eldest has a lovely head of hair, all curls. It's a treat to brush it."

The sober sense in Susan's flying words did not fail to enter deep into Rose's

vexed mind. Her foolish devotion to
Edward and Robsart had, in each case,
been harmful rather than a benefit. She
saw this clearly, and, although her heart
died within her at the thought of parting
from them, the knowledge that the
separation was, in every sense, to their
gain, gave new life to her purpose and
fresh resolution to her fainting soul.
She walked from room to room, gazing
at each piece of furniture and each poor
ornament with eyes so tender and so sad,
that Susan, not knowing why, could not
help crying.

"Oh dear!" said she, "I do hate to
see anybody go. Who can say when
they will come back?"

The trees rustled and a linnet flew out
of the hedge near the window.

"You won't forget to put crumbs on
the sill every morning," said Rose, pulling
down her thick veil; "and tell my
brother I will write to him from London.

I have put Mr. Robsart's linen in perfect order, and I have marked all his new handkerchiefs."

She gathered a little bunch of flowers from the garden, drank the tea which Susan gave her, and drove away in the pony-trap with Adam. Susan watched till she could no longer see the top of Adam's whip above the hedges. Then she went to feed the pigs, who were squealing with all their might because she had forgotten them for five minutes.

CHAPTER VI.

Some Soliloquies.

ROSE, after the manner of all women, often spoke on impulse and without due reflection, but her actions—and in this respect she differed from many of her sex —were always cautious and extremely discreet. She was not one to lose her head even in the whirlwind of adversity, and when she seemed least considerate, it would be found, on observing her conduct, that she showed much deliberation. Before she packed her box that morning, she had reasoned thus :—

" If Robsart goes to Lauderston, Edward could join him without difficulty, for his reputation is already known there and he would soon find pupils. But if I

went to Lauderston, too, it would cause
gossip, and, what is worse, we should con-
tinue the same life that we lead here.
Edward, poor soul, must learn to take
care of himself "—here she wept bitterly—
" and Robsart must forget me. I hope
he will marry a sweet, good girl, who will
love him as he deserves. But sweet, good
girls are scarce, and he must not make
his choice in a hurry." At this she grew
breathless, and, feeling like a dead thing
without a grave and with no one to close
her eyes, she fell, in a heap, on her bed.
Then she remembered that there was no
time to be lost, so she bathed and dressed,
and plaited her hair, and sang cheerful
songs in a loud voice lest Robsart—who
was eating his early breakfast in the room
below—should think she was unhappy
after their conversation of the previous
evening.

Now, therefore, that the first step was
taken and she found herself driving away,

her thoughts grew calmer and the tears
fell kindly on her face, making it young.
But she did not know this, and wondered
why a recruiting sergeant, who happened
to be at the railway, called her " Miss,"
and helped her with her luggage most
politely. He had a gallant heart for
pretty eyes and women in distress. As
the train glided from the station, Rose
looked out of the carriage window and
saw once more the little high-street with
its row of artless shops, and the gray
spire of the parish church in the distance, and the smoke of the factory,
beyond.

When Robsart returned in the afternoon, he was as little astonished as
Susan at the mere news of Rose's excur-
sion to town, but he felt that the journey
that day was not like those she had taken
before. This time she would never
return. He remembered her sorrowful
look—the trembling voice when she had

told him that they must part. She was
not a woman who would either grieve or
falter over an unmeant, unreal farewell.
There were some who coquetted with
experience, meeting heroic hours unmarked in time, calling back fugitive sorrows, conjuring up the phantom of despair, but Rose was not one of these.
Robsart's heart, sick with vexation and
disappointment, rebelled against her
austere code of honor, and the fierce
intolerance of all restraint, which, so long
as she was, at all events, near him, burnt
low, now burst forth—a vehement, three-
edged flame. She was cold, she was pitiless, she was ungrateful! He had asked
so little—merely the right to see her
daily, to sit at the same table, to lodge
under the same roof. Since that one
evening long ago had he ever uttered one
word, given a sign which the whole of
Ottley might not have heard and wit-
nessed? The mutinous thoughts, unan-

swered doubts, uneasy wonderings long
forgotten, which belonged to the early
days of his love for Rose, returned again,
and swept, like a tempest, through the
woods of his mind, stirring every feather
of the owl—his philosophy—that slept
there. He fled from the house and wandered far out into the fields, addressing
Rose in imagination, and almost persuad-
ing himself that he hated her very name.

" I do not understand your friendship," he said : " you leave me without a
word and you did not write me even a
line. How am I to believe in an affection which can disguise itself so admira-
bly? Ah, Rose, don't be deceived!
There is no love in you. You sit at your
work, thinking of fancies and fantasms
and all the melting imagery of false sentiment, till, seeing me is the dream and
not seeing me the reality. What is my
companionship to you? what is my devotion to you? what am I myself to

you? Nothing. You would rather not
talk with me—you would prefer never
meeting me. You want to flirt with my
shadow—without my knowledge and behind my back! If I misjudge you, I am
sorry. You may have religion and
thoughts about duty and thoughts about
honor, but all the religion in heaven and
all the duty preached in sermons and all
the honor described in poetry would not
make you renounce love so easily if you
were not, spirit and body, as cold as the
sea!"

He had the temperament known in
common language as steady-going, and
that poetical love which spends itself in
imagination—dissipating the soul in artificial emotions and forgetting the practical kindnesses of true friendship—seemed
to him the grossest form of insincerity.
He believed that a man should choose a
wife, protect her, provide for her, cherish
her, be faithful to her; intrigues, flirta-

tions, verse-making and serenading filled
him with an equal abhorrence, and, in his
judgment, were equally indecent. He
permitted courtship out of deference to
woman's more timorous nature and the
sublime example of Jacob, but had it
been possible, without rudeness or a too
mercantile appreciation of the value of
time, to avoid these considerations, he
would certainly have despised that cus-
tomary dalliance also. Robsart's whole
being stood rooted in affection ; with him
it was so natural and right a thing to
love, that, when Edward spoke, as he
often did, of *degrading one's aspirations
by the puny cares of marriage,* he supposed
it the mere peevishness of an invalid.
Nor could he believe that the organist
really echoed the opinions of many able-
bodied young men who exhausted their
energy denouncing the noblest responsibilities in life, seeking for wives who
would pay their debts, flattering women

who were more generous than wise. To-
day, however, in his bitterness against
Rose, he found more reasons than ill-
health for Edward's cynicism, and decided
that brother and sister had each a callous-
ness of heart which was, luckily, as rare as
it was odious.

"Ah, Rose," he continued, still easing
his despair in an imaginary conversation;
"you have read the lives of the saints
and all the imitations of Christ, which,
just because they are but imitations, are
most dangerous and misleading. Nothing in nature is solitary—go into a desert
and you will be the only lonely thing
there! The sky has its clouds and its
stars; each grain of sand is surrounded by
grains of sand! There are deep sorrows
and killing cares in life, but the encouragement and love of friends were given us
to make all difficulties bearable. To
ignore such aid is like a soldier going out
to fight the enemy singlehanded, leaving

his armor at home, despising his com-
rades and setting his commander at
defiance. We should not call such foolhardiness brave, but, on the contrary,
most insolent!"

The suspicion that he was wronging
poor Rose more than cruelly was not the
least part of his suffering. Was not her
very flight—abrupt, unkind, capricious
though it seemed—a proof, if proof were
needed, that she thought of him not too
seldom but far too much? Yet why
should she torture herself with these
scruples of conscience? why should she
lock herself in a dingy room and think
it a sin to need company, to like one
man a little better—even a great deal
better—than all others? What more natural? what so right?

And now—for a whim, a superstitious
theory of virtue—she had left him. He
determined to bear her decision for a
time, at all events, without complaint.

He felt too proud, too sore to write her
any letter or to urge her coming back.
He told his story to the evening and uttered his reproaches to the air.

CHAPTER VII.

Two Gentlemen of the Old School.

EVERY Wednesday evening, Mr. Lawrence, the curate, and Mr. Sledges, the
lawyer, used to meet at Wrestle's Farm—
sometimes for a hand at whist and sometimes for a game of chess with Robsart.
These reunions had been instituted, it was
said, for the entertainment of poor Banish,
who, when he felt in the mood, could
out-talk any man or woman in the county.
It not infrequently happened, therefore,
that the visitors left well stocked with
information for the week, and Edward
remained, sore of throat, exhausted, praying for solitude. These interruptions of
his self-contemplative life were not, however, so bad for his soul as his tongue,

and Rose, in leaving Ottley that morning, had remembered, with much comfort, the inevitable card-party of the evening. It would relieve any melancholy or resentment he might, at first, feel in learning of her departure.

When Robsart came back from his long walk, the two men were already in the parlor each with a glass of ale and both apparently waiting to be amused. Mr. Lawrence, the curate, was short, motherly in outline, over fifty, with small features and merry eyes. He was much in demand for christenings, because he held babies so well and *was not heavy-handed with the water*. The one man he found it hard to agree with was Sledges, the solicitor, who always spoke of Rome and Canterbury as though they were the parties in a divorce suit.

Sledges, himself, was all discretion, and such was his knowledge of the law, that, when it was by any means possible, he implored his clients to suffer any outrage or injustice rather than expose their grievances in Court. In appearance he was rather like a bad portrait of Macready as Richard III., and his resemblance to that tragedian cost him an immense amount of exertion in the striking of attitudes and a great deal of time in the arrangement of his hair. A windy day, for instance, disturbed the effect considerably.

Edward, when Robsart entered, was walking up and down the little room, reading a letter aloud and muttering comments, which, though inaudible as speech, betrayed, by their tone, the agitation of his mind.

" I would decide one way or the other," the curate was saying, " and then I should think no more about it. I have always found that nearly every step we take in life is to be regretted—if we once begin to wonder how many other steps might have been possible."

"Then," said Sledges, sternly, "how can you urge our friend to make a hasty decision? I never answer a letter until I have slept upon it, and, when people ask me for a reply by return of post, I always suspect that they are more eager for their own interests than mine!"

"Your calling is such," said the curate, "that you would naturally err rather on the side of caution than on the side of faith. And if one were to examine the lives directed by the Church as opposed to the lives advised by the Law, we should find, I think, that if the confident are sometimes deceived, the worldly-wise are always unhappy. And I will tell you why. There is one wisdom only, and that is heavenly. Every other kind is but a doctrine of vanity, teaching disappointment and destruction."

"If," rejoined Mr. Sledges, "I believed in prayer, I should beg to be delivered from pride of intellect!"

"And I," observed the curate, "thank God, night and morning, that, though surrounded by beings with neither true opinions nor the courage of them, I have a conviction for which I would die and for which I am perfectly willing to endure insult "—here he observed a smile on the lawyer's thin mouth—" aye, sir, and even ridicule ! "

Robsart could hardly contain his anxiety to learn the cause which had given rise to so much eloquence and wrath in his friend's learned visitors. Nor was his curiosity made less poignant when Edward, rousing himself from a dolor till that moment unutterable, made the following lament :

"It will mean shaving my beard ! "

"I do not agree with you there," said the curate.

"There again I must beg to differ with you, Mr. Lawrence," said Sledges. "The pleasures of society are only to be en-

joyed by those who conform to its regu-
lations.   If a young lady of most respectable connections invite me to her tea-table,
and, after mature consideration, I decide
to take the advantage for what it may be
worth, I do not injure that advantage by
presenting myself as its recipient in inap-
propriate habiliments !   It would not be
dignified, sir.   I may even say it would
show a want of respect for the young
lady, which her parents, should she have
any, would very properly resent."

More and more bewildered, Robsart
turned to Banish for an explanation.
The organist, without a word, gave him
the letter.   It was written in the auda-
cious hand of Miss Chloe Crecy, and
contained the hope that he, Edward,
would give her the pleasure of his company at a little tea she was giving, after
the cricket-match, on the morrow.   Mr.
Sledges and Mr. Lawrence watched Robsart's face and waited, with painful inter-

est, for his opinion. In the country, such
a small event as the attending or not
attending a tea-party has an importance
not to be estimated by those who live in
a city, and not to be exaggerated by
those who would attempt to describe it.

"What would you do when you
got there, Edward?" asked the clerk;
"would it amuse you?"

"One question at a time, please, Mr.
Robsart," said Sledges, who felt he was
protecting a client.

Edward rubbed his forehead.

"How can I tell whether it would
amuse me?" said he. "If I knew that,
I could make up my mind at once! Say
I shaved my beard, spent half an hour
driving to 'Randalls,' an hour there, half
an hour coming back, and did *not* enjoy
it, what on earth could atone to me for
the loss of time? But if, on the other
hand, I enjoyed the change, it would
really seem worth the trouble!"

"Every move in life," said Robsart, determined to preserve the solemnity of the occasion, "is an experiment. There is no such thing as an absolute certainty."

The curate held up his suave hands.

"Don't say that," he exclaimed. "Hope, at least, is sure and certain."

"Hope?" said Sledges; "the mere name is the antithesis of reason. My experience has taught me to take the gloomiest view of all subjects. That is why I am never disappointed. Things sometimes turn out better—but they are never worse—than my anticipations. If I have a cold, I am always surprised if it does not kill me. If I have to defend an honest client, I am always astonished if we win the day!"

"I note," said Mr. Lawrence, "that the possibility of divine intervention does not enter into your calculations."

"I am not so presumptuous, sir, as to

think," replied the solicitor, "that God
Almighty would either disturb the laws
of nature or suborn an English jury!
And, with no desire to be personal, I beg
to observe that all such blasphemous presumption invariably emanates from the
Church!"

Edward had now risen, and was exam-
ining his features in the small mirror
which hung over the mantelpiece.

"My sister," said he, "never liked this
beard. It would please her, I know,
to see me clean-shaven. And if she
were here, she would wish me to go to
this ridiculous entertainment at Miss
Crecy's!"

"Ah," said Mr. Lawrence, with
triumph, "now we have come to a motive which can never be barren. Think
how your actions will affect the happiness of others, and then you can always
be sure of a profitable result. If you
visit this lady out of deference to Mrs.

Arden, it cannot matter in the least whether the afternoon is dull or lively. You will have attained your point in that you have gratified the kind intention of another."

"A very dangerous theory, if I may say so," interrupted Sledges, "for, if we always observed our friends' wishes at the sacrifice of our own, we might often find ourselves committed to much that would be unwise and more that might even be immoral!"

"By no means," said Mr. Lawrence, "and in support of my denial let me quote the well-known rule attributed by Cicero to Lælius : *Ut neque rogemus res turpes, nec faciamus rogati:* that we neither require of our friends the performance of base things, nor, being requested of them, perform such ourselves. Thus, I should find no virtue in a son's committing theft at his father's command, nor should I discover any fine flavor of fidel-

ity in a wife who obeyed an evil husband.
Much misery and unhappiness has been
caused by a misapprehension and wrong
exposition of the laws of obedience."

"Aye, indeed," exclaimed Edward,
"and I am glad to hear you say so. My
poor sister would have given much to
have heard such words from a clergyman
in her youth. The poor soul was taught
such hideous rules of wifely duty, that,
for several years, she hated St. Paul, and
could not believe in a church which called
marriage a sacrament. And neither God
nor St. Paul nor marriage were at fault,
but her false teachers, who perverted
what was sacred into vileness, and what
was noble into what was ignoble!"

His eyes filled with tears, and even
Robsart, who had grown pale at the
recollection of Rose's suffering, was surprised to find that the organist had ever
given so much thought to his sister's
troubles.

"A most unfortunate affair," said Mr. Sledges. "But very few women at the present day hold such exalted ideas of duty and self-abnegation as Mrs. Arden! Her case is not a common one."

"Pardon me," said Mr. Lawrence, " I could tell you of many such cases. We clergymen know the patient souls who endure: you lawyers only meet the rebels and fighters—those who have strong friends to support them in court, and money to pay for champions! The age of chivalry, sir, is past."

Edward walked to the writing-table and sat down.

" I will go to Miss Crecy's," said he.

They all remained silent while he composed his note.

"And I will shave my beard," he added, as he fastened the envelope.

Susan carried the letter to the post, and the four men sat down to a game of whist.

CHAPTER VIII.

Introducing a Lady who Disapproved of Cynicism.

WHEN Rose reached London, she drove, in a cab, to the house of the one rich person who took an interest in her welfare —Mrs. Harrowby of Cavendish Square.

The footman who opened the door and the butler who came forward had each an air of anxiety and preoccupation which did not escape Mrs. Arden's notice. She wondered, with many misgivings, what it could mean, and, in a feverish terror, followed the elder of the two servants across the chilly hall hung with spears and the hides of beasts (from the collection of the late General Sir Frankfort Harrowby), and up the staircase.

The butler surveyed Rose's shabby gown, and, without an effort, remembered her name.

" Mrs. Arden," said he, throwing open a massive white door. The room before her was square, with low walls and a high white sloping ceiling. The paper of yellow dahlias and green leaves, the chintz of apple-blossoms which covered the sofas and chairs, and the silvery curtains embroidered with grapes and apricots, gave the prospect a garden-like appearance. The oval mirror on the dressing-table was of Pompadour design—a gilt thing of wrought butterflies, tulips, and ribbon-ends. There was a large writing-table neatly set out with a blotting-pad, silver candlesticks, and a small brazen inkstand held up by an ivory Muse. Some religious papers and *The Times* were piled up near a red morocco box of stationery. An alabaster clock stood on the mantel-piece, and above it, a mirror, in a frame

of gilt laurels and rosettes, reflected the
flaming flowers of the wall-paper.

Mrs. Harrowby was old, so she lay
propped up upon three lace-edged pillows
in an ornate French bedstead which
looked too frivolous to die in. Carved
cupids with gold wings supported the
blue silk canopy, and the coverlet was of
lilac silk worked with glittering beads
and little seed-pearls. Mrs. Harrowby
had been beautiful and she was still
admired. Many were the tales she could
tell of love and ambition, and many were
the hearts she had broken. But she had
given her own to one only and he had
failed her. Yet because Rose was his
daughter she trusted her above all women.

"My dear Rose," she exclaimed, when
she entered, "this is a great surprise. I
was on the point of writing to you.
You look wretchedly ill, but then I never
approved of your living at Ottley. Your
father would have perished in such a

place. He was a man who loved gaiety and all that was bright. Your features and eyes are like his, but in spirit you miss him completely. Your arrival in town to-day is providential. Life, however, is full of such accidents. I wish I could find time to write a book, for I am sure it would do a great deal of good. But—oh, my dear! I have had such a terrible grief. Can I bring myself to speak of it?"

"It is better," said Rose, with a sigh, "to tell a trouble than to bear it alone."

"Darrell, my maid," said Mrs. Harrowby, "Darrell, who has been my trusted servant for years, who has traveled with me and on whom I have showered many kindnesses—has suddenly left me to get married! Such selfishness has never been known. She called here in her wedding dress, and the very lace on her bonnet was a piece I had given her because it did not suit me! I wish

now that I had sent it to you. But of
course, dear, she was on the spot! I
shall take her name out of my will. She
is a heartless person."

"I suppose," said Rose, " she fell in
love !"

"Don't talk nonsense. Did you ever
see the creature? She had a figure like a
board. And now—when she is over forty
—she marries a most respectable pastry
cook. What could the man see in her?
You may depend that he is after her sav-
ings. And now I have done with maids.
I want some quiet nice soul with no idea
of bettering herself or of catching a husband—a lady, in fact, my dear. I
thought of you at once. That is why I
meant to write. I will give you seventy
pound a year, and you need not dress
much. You could put by half your salary, and save up a little for your old age.
Shall we say that everything is settled
and that you will come ? "

Rose was so astonished at what she considered direct assistance from Heaven in her hour of need, that she clapped her hands till Mrs. Harrowby herself wondered why any creature should show such extreme delight at the prospect of sharing her society, her ailments, and her humors.

"I daresay," said she, "that you will sometimes find me trying. My nerves are shocking, and I am very particular. I hope you have given up Newman's sermons, for he is not a writer I approve of. If you want Sunday reading, the new archdeacon has published some charming things on Poverty, and for week-days, there is no one like dear Sir Walter or Bernardin de Saint-Pierre. I delight in dear Saint-Pierre, and can always cry over the death of Virginia. But Thackeray—as dear old Lord Bingham once said to me—Thackeray is the enemy of the human race—a wicked cynic. My husband

would not read him in my presence!
And now, dear Rose, go to your room.
The usual one on the fifth floor near the
cistern; unpack your box, and come
back to me directly. I shall go down to
dinner to-night, for Colonel Thompson
and Sir Harry Blythe are coming, and I
should like you to rearrange the neck of
my ruby velvet. You have such excellent taste!"

Now all this she said in guile to try
Rose's heart, for Mrs. Harrowby was a
woman who played as many characters as
Proteus had shapes. But she had never
cried over the death of Virginia, and she
hated the new archdeacon.

As Rose climbed the stairs to the attic,
her feet seemed wings, and, when she
entered that narrow room, it looked, to
her grateful sight, the turret chamber in
a fairy palace. Yet the walls were gray,
and the curtains at the one small window, malignant saffron. In one corner a

wooden bedstead offered uneasy rest,
and, facing it, a tin stand, with a basin
and jug, trembled in the draught of air
which crept under the door and up
through the gaping boards. A mouse,
as Rose came in, glided from the cup-
board to the hearth, where, with a squeal,
it disappeared. Rose placed the white
flowers she had brought from Ottley on
the mantelpiece, and, when she bent over
their petals to smell them, she caught
their pallor, and they, her tears. When
she lifted her face, however, a breeze
stirred the curtain aside and the glad sun
touched her sad cheeks. Her lips found
a song to sing: the pain in her heart
fell asleep. She unlocked her little box
and discovered, well pressed down on her
best bonnet, half a large seed-cake and a
bottle of balsam for colds, which the
thoughtful Susan had thrust under the
lid at the last moment. These set her
laughing, and, when she scattered the

cake-crumbs on the window-sill for wan-
dering birds, she kissed her hand toward
Susan at Ottley and looked up at the
great, great sky which saw them both.
And, as she remembered this, she seemed
no longer separated from her friends, for
she sent her soul into the vast cloudland
where eternal day and eternal night melt
together and are one Dawn.

CHAPTER IX.

Concerning Heroes, Sorrow and a Horse.

IT wanted but two hours to the time fixed for Miss Crecy's party, when Susan laid out Edward's clean shirt upon his bed and placed his shoes, well cleaned by Adam, on the hearth-rug.

"They use more starch than elbow-grease at Blackett's," said she to the little maid who assisted her, "and Blue enough to eat away the sails of a fishing smack! I will put one of the shirts I washed last week by the side of this, tuck some pink paper down the front, and I lay you a penny Mr. Edward will take it for the one he sent to be *falamered-up* by those husseys at the steam laundry! Men are all the same. They always think that

something they are going to get is better
than what they have got! He has shaved
his beard, too—a bit of foolishness I
don't hold with. I knew a gentleman—
he was in the army—as couldn't please
his wife no way—she was an invalid lady
that wrote poetry, poor soul—so he cut
off his moustache and came upon her sudden. But she said it was only changing a
monster she knew for a monster she didn't
know, and she got colder than ever. He
was buried at Kensal Green, and she had
a lovely monument put over him—an
angel weeping by a cypress, with one finger
pointing up to heaven. And I never
see angels now but I think of Mr. Barn-
aby's moustache. Now, come along, do;
you mustn't stand there talking all day."

So she seized the listening maiden by
the arm and drove her to the kitchen,
where she rated her well for her idleness
and instructed her further in the follies
of mankind.

Meanwhile, Edward came home, stroking his shorn chin, a handsome feature, and whistling the tune of

> "What is love? 'tis not hereafter :
> Present mirth hath present laughter ;
> What's to come is still unsure.
> In delay there lies no plenty.
> Then come kiss me, sweet-and-twenty,
> Youth's a stuff will not endure ! "

He had been for a swim in the river, and was trembling pleasantly from the exercise, or at the anticipation of seeing a shirt ironed to his taste. He bounded up the narrow staircase, burst into his bedroom, and lo! there were the linen garments, as he had hoped to find them, spread out.

"Ah!" he cried, choosing at a glance the one which had the bravest show of pink paper, "at last, a decent collar—and cuffs one can show. Who would grudge eightpence for a polish like this?"

He whistled four merry airs while he

dressed, but he was silent for three-quarters of an hour while he chose and arranged his necktie. His trousers, his coat, and waistcoat were of dark-blue serge, he had a new straw hat and his hair had been cut that morning.

"La, sir!" said Susan, running out of the larder as he descended the stairs, "they won't know you! And does the shirt answer?" she added, in a wheedling tone.

"You see," said he, not wishing to hurt her feelings, "they have every sort of machine at the steam laundry."

"Fancy that!" said she, "and yet my work's the best!"

"What do you mean?" said he, observing a droll reflection of himself in a metal dish-cover which hung on the kitchen wall.

"That's one as I washed that you're wearing now, sir," said she, gravely, with a long side wink at the chair in which her husband usually sat. "I am glad you are pleased with it," she continued; "but you *do* look hot! The fire does catch one at this time of the year. I've ordered in a bushel of that pink paper—it's as cheap as dirt, and gentry is always fond of it. I once knew a lady who wouldn't touch a morsel of hog's-flesh unless you called it ham and dinked it round with a frill!"

Edward struck the door with his walking-stick and wiped his brow.

"Why," said he, "is Adam so long with that pony?"

Arabella, the pony, was very old, and looked as though she were made of wicker-work covered with horse-hide. When they tightened her girths all her skin would wrinkle and her bones, like osiers, would creak and bend. Yet she could canter up a hill with the best and trot almost as evenly as a young mule. Adam now led her forth—with a scarlet rose under each ear—from the stable, and Susan ran to drag the cart from its shed. When all was prepared, the organist climbed into the vehicle, and Georgiana, the little maid, packed his rug, his mackintosh, and a basket to be filled at the grocer's, into the box behind. Then Edward took the whip and the moist reins and touched Arabella on the head.

"Mind her new rosette," said Susan, as she opened the yard gate.

Then, at the familiar sound of the lifted latch, Arabella struck the attitude of speed, and trotted slowly down the road through the meadow, with her load and the young man.

Now when they were come within sight of the great iron gate of "Randalls," Edward halted at "The Bear and Breeches," renowned for its bad ale—an inn at which Arabella had never once in her life so much as paused at. Here, however, he left the indignant animal,

who was led into a yard, unharnessed by
a drowsy ostler, and put to rest in a
stall, near a litter of mongrel puppies,
and usually occupied, as was evident by
the aroma and some scattered fur, by a
gray donkey. Then Edward took his
mackintosh from the cart, and, promis-
ing to return for Arabella before sunset,
he went out again on the high-road toward " Randalls." And when he reached
the entrance, the gates already stood
open, for a carriage, full of young ladies
with flowery hats, was passing through,
while the lodge-keeper touched his cap,
and his wife bade her five children—who
were staring as still as sunflowers in a
row—keep quiet. Edward lingered a
little lest the dust sent flying by the
wheels should soil his coat, but he bowed
to the damsels, who, in return, smiled
from under their veils, and they wondered among themselves who he could
be, whether he was some squire's son or

an officer from the barracks at Lauderston—he looked so new and strange without his beard.

When he came to the archway before
the house, he rested a moment and surveyed the bronze dragons on either side,
who sat, each with an uplifted paw,
keeping guard over the coat of arms, the
drawn sword, the shield and plumed hel-
met, which belonged to Mr. Crecy, the
brewer. The mansion was built of white
stone, and there were glass windows to
the wide door—that one might see the
marble hall within, where a fountain
played, and statues of nymphs from Italy
stood on pedestals and vasty pictures
from the Royal Academy adorned the
staircase. No garden was in sight, but
only high walls topped with spikes, which
ran from the archway to the façade,
forming a square courtyard. Edward
sighed heavily as he now advanced to
pull the brass bell, and he thought of

the ever-open door at the farm, and of
the watchful geese who were all that was
needed to defend its threshold from
intruders.

A footman in a brown and yellow liv-
ery answered his summons, and a butler,
pale and pompous, conducted him
through the conservatory on to the lawn,
where sat Miss Crecy and her mother,
and the young ladies with the flowery
hats and several young gentlemen in
white flannel, drinking tea and feeding
fat dogs, who were not hungry, with
plum-cake. Then Edward considered
whether he should take to his heels and
so make an end of all ceremony, or be
well-mannered and show a sad countenance like the seemly young men in
white flannel. But as he turned these
thoughts within his mind, he caught his
foot in a croquet hoop, and he took this
as a sign from the angels that he should
stay. So he lifted his eyes valiantly and

straightway met those of Miss Crecy—
which were as calm and blue as sap-
phires, but more admiring.

"How wonderful!" thought he, "for,
although I tripped over the hoop and
must have looked an ass, I no longer feel
that I was foolish to have come here.
Yet my heart is spinning in my side and
my knees are bending under me."

Miss Crecy's locks were tawny and her
cheeks had the pink of apple blossoms.
Her nose was as straight and her chin
was as pointed and her hair as beauti-
fully smooth as a bride's in a fashion
book, and Edward thought that he had
never beheld so wifely a person, although
they had met many times before that
day. But the whole world had looked
different to him since the shaving-off of
his beard.

When Miss Crecy's hand touched his
in greeting, he became happier yet, and
followed her with a glad spirit even to

her mother's chair. That lady, remembering he was but an organist, smiled upon him cautiously, and begged him to take a seat between the curate's wife and her aged aunt. So he sat down as he was told, and silence fell upon them all, till one young girl who was engaged to be married, and who was therefore more daring than the rest, knew him by his eyebrows and his white hands.

"La!" said she, "'tis Mr. Banish! I couldn't make him out!"

At this the whole party burst out laughing, and, under cover of the general merriment, every couple found an opportunity to stroll away, some toward the bowling-ground, and others among the trees and flower-beds. Edward, who was no laggard, seized his chance and Miss Crecy's croquet mallet.

"Shall we play?" said he.

The maiden was too courteous to refuse such an invitation from her own

guest. They crossed the lawn together
and achieved two games, neither decisive,
for both combatants were unwilling either
to win or lose, so perfect was their match
in good-humor and prowess.

Yet, after a little, Edward looked at
the leafy woods hard by which led to the
apple orchard, and he thought how pleasant it would be to go there, farther than
the eyes of the curate's wife and Miss
Crecy's admirable mother could reach.
So he spoke cunning words about the
heat of the day; but Miss Crecy knew
all, and she dropped her mallet, saying:

"I see my cousin beckoning from the
arbor. Shall we join them?"

Therefore they went that way, till, as
they drew near their destination, Edward
saw, at a long distance down a side-path,
some mushrooms growing in a ring—as
though, as the story goes, fairies had
danced there. Whereupon he suggested
that they should examine the rare spot—

to which his fair companion sweetly agreed. The expedition produced a very pretty conversation about elves and witchcraft and old country tales of love and omens.

"Yet there are people who declare," exclaimed the maiden, " that these things are past, and many more doubt that they ever were at any time. If one could be frank in this life, I daresay we could all tell a story as strange and romantic as any you read of in books."

This she said in her wile to find out whether he had a secret grief. But Edward was ashamed to own that he had for his part no romantic experience to boast of, so he just sighed as though his heart would break and looked more sorrowful than a weeping willow.

"I know," said he, "a story which ended before it began."

"There was never such a story in this world," said she.

"Dear lady," said he, "you must take my word for it."

"There is a way out of every difficulty," said she.

"Aye," said he, "into a fresh one!"

"I find a certain hopelessness," said she, "in your philosophy."

"I never take up arms against the truth," said he.

"What is truth," said she, "but a thing we ourselves make out of hearsays?"

"I could wish it were no more," said he.

"Then tell me the story," said she, "I should understand——"

"Quite well," said he. "You have a heart."

"More head," said she, with a gasp, "more head, I assure you!"

She paled : she reddened.

"A woman's kindness," said he, "and a man's deliberation!"

"I often regret my excessive calm-
ness," said she, trembling from head to
foot. "It might, to some, look selfish."

"Never—to me," said he. "I think it
queenly!"

"You use such words!"

"I think aloud."

"A dangerous habit."

"Not when I am with—a friend!" and
he heaved another great sigh.

"I, too," said she, not to be outdone,
"I, too, have had trouble!"

"You?"

"Your story first!"

"You make me forget it!" And as
he made this answer, he inly laughed, for
he had no story to tell.

"I make you forget it?" she said.
"How is that?"

"I find it so much harder to bear your
grief than my own. I pictured you al.
ways happy!"

"I do not complain."

"Because you are majestic!"

"I am awake for hours at night," said she. "I cry. Would you believe it?"

"From your eyes—no!"

"Ah," said she, "one can cry without tears."

"True,"said he, "all things have a resurrection except the emotions. They are born—they die—they never return. A happiness or a despair once gone is a phantom for ever."

"My friend," said she, "we soon grow accustomed to solitude of soul, and, after all, there is a dignity in solitariness! Sympathy makes one cling to life: isolation exalts us to the sublime!"

At this point one or both of them stumbled over a fallen bird's nest, and their shoulders touched. Whereupon Edward stooped to pick up the cause of that pleasing accident. And he found three newly-fledged starlings in the nest —two dead, but one still living. And the girl, pale with pity, took it from him, and wrapt it about with her soft handkerchief, and placed it, without prudery or ado, in her breast—an act which seemed to the young man so tender and so gracious that he could no longer deceive her kindness by a false woe.

"If I have ever felt unhappy," said he, "my selfishness—not my fate—has been at fault. There has been no romance in my past, and I have never seen but one woman I could love."

"Then to be honest," said she, getting red, "I was never once awake all night in my life, and as for love or sorrow, I know nothing of either!"

At this they laughed, but, by and by, sighed.

"And have you never met any one—" said he.

"How could I tell till he asked me?" said she.

"I am asking," he said.

"Good heavens!" she exclaimed, "you must give one time. On so short an acquaintance, too! What would you think of me if I said yes? Not that I could. For how should I know one way or the other? Yet I can well believe in love at first sight."

"It is then or never," cried Edward. "One look is enough!"

So she looked at him, and in a honeyed silence they retraced their steps, which now seemed strewn with sweet remembrances of their wonderful journey.

Meanwhile, Robsart had returned home from the factory, and as he found the sitting-room desolate because Rose was not there, he went into the kitchen. Then Susan told him of her trick with the shirt, and of Arabella's new rosettes, and how Edward had left in such haste that he forgot to say at what time he would like his supper. But Robsart's heart was dull, and he soon walked out on

to the road, where now, at every cottage
gate, a girl or an old woman stood watching for the postman. Some, as he passed,
looked away from him sadly, and some
pretended not to heed him, and a few
blushed red with pride to find that they
had not been forgotten. Robsart followed the man at a little distance, and
when he saw him making for the farmhouse, he feared to stop him lest he
should hear too soon that the letter was
not for himself. So he loitered by the
hedges, watching the grasshoppers and
the butterflies and the spiders' webs.
And presently he beheld a pony in the
distance, walking slowly, with neither a
rider nor a harness, and, by her knock-
knees and shape, he knew her to be Arabella. At the sight of him she whinnied,
and, as he ran to meet her, her eyes held
a rage he could not fathom.

"Arabella," said he, in deadly terror,
"where is Edward?"

She tossed her head, and feigned to look at some crows who were feeding in a meadow close at hand.

"You must turn back with me and find him," said Robsart.

But at this she lay down flat on the road till her very eyelashes touched the dust.

"You are a wicked girl!" said he.

As she had been old now for many years, this flattered her vanity, and after a seeming resistance, she relented, rose up, and suffered him to lead her back towards East Ottley and "The Bear and Breeches."

Robsart looked anxiously about him as he went, hoping yet dreading to find some trace of Edward and the missing cart, but they saw neither chick nor man till they reached the cross-roads, where a recruiting sergeant—none other, in fact, than the one who had helped Rose into the train—appeared to be studying the

mile-post, as though he could not decide
which direction to take. But in reality
he had his mind on Robsart, for his
height and his build were soldierly, and
he thought it a shame that such a fine
figure of a man should be leading old
ponies through empty lanes.

" Have you, by any chance," said
Robsart, as he came up, "seen a trap by
the wayside? or have you met a young
man in a blue serge suit, good looking
and quick walker, coming from East
Ottley ?"

" No," said the sergeant, "but I am
bound there now, and, as I am a stranger
in these parts, I should be glad of your
company. That's been a pretty animal
in her day," added he, patting Arabella
on the neck ; " not a bit of vice about
her, I can see, and it wouldn't surprise
me to hear that she had carried many an
officer at polo. Our colonel has a pony
that couldn't touch her—as she may

have been once, so to speak—and he wouldn't sell her for eighty pound."

"This is really very odd," replied Rob-sart, "for, as a matter of fact, this pony belonged to my mother's brother who is a captain in the 21st Hussars. He is now in India, but he was—and may be still—a famous polo player."

"I knew I couldn't be mistaken, sir," said the sergeant, who was nevertheless greatly astonished. "Style is style, and although I say it myself, nothing comes up to the army for putting men and beasts into the right trim. God bless me! I've seen many young fellers with no more pluck nor manliness than so many tins of meat, who, inside a twelve-month, have turned out downright credits! I can tell you, sir, that going about the country as I do, I see enough to make any sensible man heave his heart up. What sort of life do these young fellers lead? Twiddling on the banjo,

singing like professionals, reading tommy-
rot in the newspapers, sitting about the
house like a parcel of old women? If
they take part in some fiddling cricket-
match, you might think, to hear 'em talk,
that they were Ajaxes and Achillums!
If they play croquet with a couple of
gals, they are ready to drink the sea dry
for thirst. Wet feet will send 'em to bed
for a fortnight, and after a day on their
legs they are ready to drop! Then some
of 'em fall in love every new moon, and
instead of saying to the gal, ' Stay here,
my dear, till I have knocked about a bit
and can keep a home together' ; they
court first this one and then that one—
worse than an old gander my mother once
had, as could never make up his mind.
He was a rum character—that ; one in
ten thousand I should say—for a gander
will stop true to one mate all his life.
I could tell you a tale about a gander as
would put many a man to the blush."

"Pray tell it," said Robsart.

"Well," said the sergeant, "he was a
fine handsome bird with a nasty temper,
and my mother, being a careful woman,
gave him four geese. One was a sweet
pretty creature, all white and with them
feathers which curl. But he wouldn't be
even civil to her. Another was plain
white, without much show, yet a young
brisk thing, bright in the eye and all that.
Do you think he even noticed her? Not
he! I've seen that poor thing with her
feelings so hurt that she could scarcely
eat. And another was gray and white,
rather lanky, but what one might call
elegant. I've known him to talk to her
—but that's all. The one he liked was a
common gray goose, small and meek,
with a nice sort of face, yet nothing wonderful. And he couldn't bear her out of
his sight. He would peck at all the
others to keep 'em from feeding while
she picked out the bits to her fancy.

And just because the white one with curled feathers was prettier than she was, he treated her with cruel spite— just out of loyalty, as you may say, and for fear his favor*ite* should be jealous! So my mother had no choice but to kill the little gray goose—for, said she, who could afford to encourage such nonsense? Women are very heartless toward females. And when that gander saw his mate hanging up in the larder, all plucked for selling, he walked off to the pond and he ducked his head I don't know how many times; and when he came ashore about sunset, he had all gone to nothing. And he used to stand for hours under the tree watching the gate she used to sit by. Then the three geese would try to cheer him up, and he hadn't the heart left to chase them away; but they never got a smile from him. We waited a month, and his temper grew worse and worse. He was always watching the gate and

hissing at all petticoats, even those hung
out to dry. So at last my mother had
to kill him too, and she bought another
gander. That's a true story, and a dozen
could swear to it."

"I can well believe it," said Robsart,
" for I live on a farm."

"Indeed," said the sergeant; "do you
think of settling down in that line?"

"Oh no," said Robsart, "my work is
in the factory. I am a book-keeper. But
finish what you were telling me about
the men you see. I have often thought
myself that long courtships and country amusements were very unsatisfactory."

"Unsatisfactory is not the word," said
the sergeant, "ruination is nearer! Why,
if a man can't tell the very moment he
claps his eye on a woman whether she
suits him, I wouldn't give much for his
backbone. And if he will put up with
any makeshift instead of her, he's a poor

stick. Mind you! I am speaking of marriage. A bit of a lark now and again is another thing and all very well in its way, but your wife is your wife wherever you go, whether you sling her on your arm or whether you leave her at home— she's bone of your bone; and if she's the right sort, you can't go very far wrong, I'm blowed if you can. And I've watched many married men in my time. It's the men that have to fight who think the most of their families, and it's the men that go away that the women is most pleased to see come back. If I had my way every man should serve his term in the army. It stands to reason that we cannot all be soldiers, for some must watch the land, and some must be scholars, and some must keep shops, and some, on account of the women, must be doctors and parsons. There are many callings, as we all know; but for a young, strong feller with no ties and no especial

duties as a civilian—well, I leave it to
you to say what *he* ought to do."

Now the sergeant was a guileful soul,
and, in telling the gander's story, he
had learned—what he already suspected—
from Robsart's countenance, that he had
just such another bird walking by his
side.

"Lor' bless yer soul," said he, "if
you've got anything on your mind—(I
know what it is—I myself have been—well
there, fit to blooming well hang myself)
—a barracks is just the place for you.
You get taken out of yourself in no time.
It is not an easy life, of course—what's
the good of telling lies?—but young
chaps are all the better for a bit of hardship. And you get an idea of life—you
see a thing or two—and if you have
trouble you are soon taught how to bear
it; and if pleasure comes, you soon
learn how to enjoy yourself without
playing the fool."

And then he began to tell of his adventures in the East, and all that he saw and all that he suffered, and how he fought the Sikhs at Goojat and how he was quite ready to fight them all over again to-morrow.

"The first time I was in action," said he, " I was little more than a drummer-boy. When the rumpus began, we didn't feel so bad, but presently I saw a Highlander shot through the heart, and then I knew what I was in for. Just to tell you what men are, there was one feller there who wanted to run away; and the captain, who was beginning to look queer himself, pulled up at that, as bold as a lion. 'If you stir,' says he, ' I'll shoot you!' And that very chap as wanted to desert started in as if he was half mad, and got rewarded for distinguished service. Fight! he fought like a demon. He struck out six ways for Sunday. He gave 'em a treat, and no mistake about it! We are never hard on Nature in the army: we expect men to be human. Every one is timid at first: and them as pretends to be so used to it all, as it were, is the biggest cowards of the lot!"

Robsart, as he listened, felt his heart stir within him, for he was getting very weary of his desk at the cotton works.

"Now, if I was a young man and had my time over again," continued the sergeant, " I should go into the Lancers. You get two good horses, as handsome a uniform as any one could wish, and board and lodging fit for a king! It's life—that's what it is! And advancement is wonderful quick—one way and another. You've just got to obey orders, and there you are! No responsibility and nothing to worry about. And to see the Lancers coming down a road, full trot, is the prettiest sight in the world: the gals lean half a mile out of their windows to look at 'em! There was one young gentleman as took my advice, and, without giving names, I may say he will soon get his majority! He was—as you might be—a gentleman born; but he was down on his luck and working for his living. Between you and me, he was looking rather lovin' at his razors of a morning. And one day we happened to cross over to Portsmouth together, and, if you please, I saw him hanging over the the ship's side, with a precious queer pair of eyes in his head. 'Now then,' says I, 'buck up!' And he bust out crying like a child—fit to break his heart; yet that young blubberer is now one of the general's A.D.C.'s, and as plucky a chap as you'd find in the whole army. But blubbering proves nothing. It's only human nature."

At this moment, Edward, swinging his racquet, and staring up at the sky, appeared in sight.

"Thank God!" said Robsart, "for I

didn't know what to think. Where's the
cart?"

"The cart," said Edward, "is at 'The
Bear and Breeches.' That beastly animal," he added, with a look at Arabella,
"must have walked out of the stables
while the ostler was asleep. He told me
that the airs she gave herself were past all
bearing. But let us go back for the trap
and drive home together."

He did not wonder to see Robsart walking with a stranger, for, in those lonely
parts, one was always glad of a comrade.

So Edward joined the clerk and the
sergeant, and the three, with the pony,
marched on to East Ottley. Edward,
however, seemed in no mood to talk or to
listen, and he still stared at the sky, even
while the sergeant told stories of heroism
and adventure. But Robsart was full of
thought, and when they at last reached
the inn, he called the sergeant aside.

"Give me the shilling," said he; for it

was at a time when they still gave the Queen's shilling to recruits."

"Right you are!" said the sergeant, with a heavy oath, "You are the man for my money!"

CHAPTER X.

In which Susan has Cause to Remember Rose Arden.

ABOUT this hour, Susan was standing at the door of the farm, watching for Edward and Robsart. The stars were now coming out, the fowls had gone to roost, and it was long past supper time.

"I feel sad-like," said she to Georgiana, who stood by her side, "for I saw the new moon through glass, and when I do that I always hear a bit of bad news."

"And I," said Georgiana, "dreamt last night of a white horse, and there's no sign worse than that."

"Hold your tongue, do," said Susan. "I haven't patience with such foolery. And, well I never! here comes old

Mother Venus. What ever does she want now? creeping along the road as if she was looking out for a Moses or an Aaron! She might bide at home in the evening at her time of life."

"La!" said Georgiana, beginning to weep, for she was watery-hearted, " she's croi-ing (crying), poor soul, that's what she's doing. What's she croi-ing vur, I wonder? And she looks the breathing image of my old grandmother as lives at Ottley Major, and has the 'sipelas. Yet Mrs. Venus ain't so old as granny by a good twenty year."

"How are you, Mrs. Venus?" said Susan, as the woman approached ; "none the worse, I hope, for the flies? They are something cruel this year."

" Oh, Susan," said Mrs. Venus, with a dreadful sob, " I don't mind nothing now. My Arthur's been and 'listed!"

" What!" said Georgiana, leaning against the door-post and turning the color of lead.

"He's been and 'listed," said Mrs. Venus. "The sergeant got him on with drink and a pack of lies, and he took the shilling and he's done for. To think he should have come as low as that! My Arthur! And the sergeant took him off to the doctor's—my Arthur as never had a day's illness in his life—to see whether he was fit to be chopped up and cut about by foreigners and the blackies!"

And she threw her apron over her head and rocked herself to and fro. But Georgiana could not cry now, for she loved Arthur, and she sat huddled up on the step, seeing nothing.

"That sergeant is as sly as a fox," said Susan; "he ought to be ashamed of hisself bringing such disgrace into a widow woman's family. And Arthur should have had more sense than to listen to him."

"It ain't in my Arthur," said Mrs. Venus, "to do such a shameful thing of

his own free will. He doesn't see the
disgrace, bless you! he talks about fight-
ing for his country as if he was some
Dook in parliament! It's like driving off
to the Union in a wagonette and pair—
that's what it is. Just see how I've
worked and scraped to 'prentice that
boy to the undertaking! Mr. Harden
was only saying the other day that he
never had a lad with such a knack at
lining coffins. He's so handy with his
fingers-like. It's the disappointment I
look at, for I was hoping to see him set up
for himself later on and take care of me
when I am too old to take care of him.
And instead of that, the last coffin he
lined will just do for my burial. This
is my death-blow, and no mistake. I
sha'n't hold my head up again. If his
father was alive, he'd break every bone
in his body—he was a very hasty man
was my poor husband. My Arthur's
been and 'listed," she said again, lifting

up her voice like a howling dog; " my Arthur's been and 'listed."

"Now don't take on like that, Mrs. Venus," said Susan; " whatever is God's will is for the best, as my poor mother— now dead and gone—used to say."

"Aye," replied Mrs. Venus, " and right enough, she is dead and gone for all her wise words, and whether that's for the best, the worms can tell better than I can! God's will ain't my will— that's all I know. Oh, Georgina, you knew my poor boy—you used to walk out with him. Ain't it heart-break-ing?"

Georgiana forced her handkerchief into her mouth for fear she would weep aloud, and Mrs. Venus passed on, stumbling over the stones as she went and shedding big tears.

"What's the use of giving way?" said Susan, swallowing her pity; "I've got to think of my husband. He can't

bear to see my face all blubbered with
crying. It upsets him for a week. But
you take and draw a jug of ale and carry
it into Mrs. Venus's with my love. And
the broth as I made to-day might warm
her up a bit. Pour some of it in the
large basin. Upon my word, you can't
stand at your own door for a breath of
fresh air but you see some poor creature
in trouble. Look sharp, now, and keep
your wits about you. What's Arthur to
you, I should like to know, or fifty Ar-
thurs? At your age, I never thought of
the men—I wasn't in such a hurry to
make myself miserable, I wasn't. Walking out with Arthur Venus! They're a
good-for-nothing lot those Venuses—
root and branch. You let me catch you
crying about him—that's all. I'm thank-
ful to God he's been and 'listed, or you
would have been in a pretty trouble, I'll
warrant. There's more love than marriage in this courting, my girl."

So Georgiana went softly away to the cellar and drew the ale, as she was told, for Mrs. Venus. But her body fell against the wall at every other step, and her heart felt like a grindstone at her side.

Susan still remained at the threshold, looking again and again up the road for Robsart and Edward, till, at last, she heard wheels on the long meadow road.

" Here they be," she called out to Adam, who had been smoking his pipe in the kitchen, " but Arabella sounds a bit lame. She's getting old now for these sort of outings. And you mark my words, Mr. Edward won't tell us what they had for tea at Miss Crecy's nor nothing he saw. Talking to him is like turning the handle of a locked door—you may turn and turn but you get nowhere! "

When the cart came in sight, Susan grew as pale as death, for there was the sergeant sitting on the back seat.

"Adam," said she, in a quiet voice, "I've got a feeling that Betty and her calf ain't comfortable. Will you creep round to the barn and bide there with her till I come? But mind you stay till I come and close the door well after you—for the air to-night is very searching."

Then, when Adam had gone, she went forth, with all the courage of a tigress guarding her young, to meet the sergeant and offer him a glass of ale.

"Upon my heart and life, Mr. Edward," said she, "I thought you had run away with Miss Crecy. And there's Mr. Robsart who wouldn't touch a morsel without you. Good-evening, sergeant. The world ain't treating you badly, judging you by your looks!"

The sergeant saluted her politely and showed all his fine white teeth.

"I've come to rob you, missis," said he, "of one of your young gentlemen."

"I want none of your larks!" said Susan, losing her voice.

"It's quite true, Susan," said Robsart. "I've enlisted."

The woman glanced at Edward, who was standing with his lips set close and his eyes swimming in tears.

"O my God!" said she. "Poor Mrs. Arden!"

"Look alive!" growled the sergeant, "look alive! It's all for his own good; there's no one to be sorry for, and there's no bones broken!"

"Oh, Mr. Robsart," said Susan, in spite of him, "how ever could you ha' done such a thing?"

"Because he's a man," said the sergeant; "because he's sick and tired of women's mews and miaus; because he's got a pair of arms and legs; because he can listen to common sense; because he wasn't born to set down 'ought and carry one' all day! That's why, if you want to know."

Susan wiped her face with her apron, and began to unharness Arabella.

"My poor gal," said she, "this is the heaviest load as you ever brought to my door."

"Allow me, ma'am," said the sergeant, assisting with the buckles, while his sly pale eyes came peeping through their lids like the moon between clouds.

Edward went into the house and Robsart followed him. There they met Georgiana, sobbing in the passage, with the jug of ale and the basin of broth for Mrs. Venus.

"Oh, sir," cried Georgiana, "have you heard the dreadful news? Arthur Venus with the curly hair has been and 'listed. And I'm croi-ing because his mother croïd. I can't bear to see anybody croï—I can't.''

And she crept out the back way among the bushes so that Susan should not see her tears.

CHAPTER XI.

Chaste Conversation Coupled with Fear.

THE next afternoon, Mrs. Triptree, the Vicar's wife, sallied forth on foot to call on her friend, Mrs. Crecy. She wore her best green silk with the brown stripes, and her bonnet had four strings—two to tie under her chin, and two, of broad, figured ribbon, to fly in the wind. Her face was round and red, but she had a white sharp nose; her eyes were as black and lustreless as currants, and her lips were like the mouthpiece of a trumpet. She bore in her hand a small silk parasol, edged with long fringe and mounted on a long ivory stick. Her gloves were of white kid with two buttons. On one wrist she wore a gold bracelet; on the other, a band of black velvet. And thus she came to the great front door of "Randalls," where, it so happened, Mrs. Crecy was alighting from her high barouche drawn by gray horses.

"Good-afternoon, Mrs. Triptree," said she. "I would not have missed you for a sovereign ! I hope your daughters are none the worse for my party yesterday, although, to be sure, I gave them but a very simple tea."

"Ah, we all know your simples, Mrs. Crecy," said Mrs. Triptree, "tipsy cake and hot-house grapes and champagne cup, and every sort of tart. Upon my word, there is no one in Ottley—no, nor from all I can hear, in the whole county—that keeps such a table. The Colonel's wife gives a very poor spread—such a spread as you wouldn't set before your own family !"

"La !" said Mrs. Crecy, "and I've heard that her god is her stomach. The longer I live, Mrs. Triptree, the less heed I give to gossip. But come into the garden where it is cool and tell me your news."

"Oh, my dear!" said Mrs. Triptree, as they crossed the hall, "I look to you for that. We are very dull at the Vicarage just now—unless some things I heard this morning should happen to be true. But there! what is one to believe? I don't like to mention names."

"Nor do I," said Mrs. Crecy, "for, upon my word, the servants have ears in every tree. But does the name you were thinking of begin with 'A'?"

"One might be said to begin with an 'A,'" replied Mrs. Triptree.

"And I'll be bound it has an 'R' in it."

"To be sure there is more than one 'R' in the story, Mrs. Crecy."

"And that other 'R' is the first letter of a name ending in 'T'?"

" 'Tis really too bad of you," said Mrs.
Triptree, " you are worse than a judge."

" Mrs. A. has gone to town and Mr. R.
has enlisted!" said Mrs. Crecy. "Cook
heard it at crack of dawn this morning
from the milk-boy. You could have
blown me away like a thistle when she
told me. 'Well, I never,' said I, 'well, I
never!' Just like that. 'What does the
Vicar think?' I thought to myself. 'I
would give five shillings to know what
the Vicar says to this.'"

"The Vicar," said Mrs. Triptree, "has
always been of my opinion that Mrs.
Arden is a woman with the nicest ideas
of propriety. When do you see her
decked out? Her best black silk is her
wedding dress dyed. I heard that from
Susan. When does she put her veil up
in church? When does she go out before
the sermon? When does she invite cu-
rates or married men to tea? When do
you find her gossiping at street corners?

She's a very nice woman, indeed, and if
she's plain, that's not her fault, and perhaps it's her blessing. And if she looks
thirty-nine—if she's a day—it may be her
age or it may be trouble—that is neither
here nor there. I don't as a rule trust
auburn hair, but we should always hope
for the best."

"And I can hear nothing said against
Louis Robsart," observed Mrs. Crecy.
"You may depend, however, that there
is more in this enlisting than we think.
Say what you will, it looks very odd,
Mrs. Triptree."

"Nothing would surprise me," said
Mrs. Triptree, "but as he went last night
to Lauderston and he has chosen foreign
service, we may take it that what may
have been, will be no more!"

"And who knows what may have
been?" said Mrs. Crecy.

"Who, indeed?" said Mrs. Triptree.
"I was thinking—but why say it?

What a lovely view you have from this seat. To watch the world from such a corner, Mrs. Crecy, one would swear it was all virtue. The blue sky and the peaceful cows. Heaven above and happy animals, made by the Creator, basking in the sun. A pretty, pretty sight! Do you get your meat from Lauderston, or do you still kill your own?"

"We kill our own," replied Mrs. Crecy, "and if you would accept a sirloin of beef—the best (though that's not much) that poor 'Randalls' can offer—I should be most happy."

"La!" said Mrs. Triptree, "one would think I had been hinting, whereas such a thought never came into my head! I vow it isn't safe to admire the least object in your presence. The Vicarage is already much beholden to you."

"Be that as it may," replied Mrs. Crecy, "where gratitude is, I say, there it's worth your while to drop favors. Not that I am able to do all I could wish, for, what with the house and the stables, the servants' hire and keep, what with the grounds and victuals, what with clothes for one's back, works of art and the cellar—a thousand pound seems no more than a sixpenny bit. Yet you are wel. come to the beef, Mrs. Triptree—most welcome. I hope, as the old saying goes, it will be cut and come again. But what were you thinking about poor Mrs. Ar. den?"

"La! I have clean forgotten. Ah well, 'tis all for the best. A tale loses noth. ing by being repeated—be as careful as you please. A quart of doubt to an ounce of truth is the safest brew. Yet— though I never spoke again—I should have to say my say if a question were put to me on oath. If I were put on my oath, Mrs. Crecy, and any one were to ask me, ' Have you any reason to suspect thus and so?' or, 'Do you think that a

certain person is this, that, or the other?'
I should feel bound to tell the truth."

"And what would you say, Mrs. Triptree?"

"I should say, 'Well, be it far from me
to judge, but if I know a pigeon from a
beehive, that young man is in love with
Edward Banish's sister!' It all points
to it, Mrs. Crecy. She, being a God-fear-
ing, superior person, leaves Ottley, and he,
in a fit of pique, enlists. 'Tis as clear as
anything in a book. There was never a
clearer case. And that reminds me. My
girls were saying that you had young
Banish here yesterday. That was most
condescending, I am sure. He owes you
a great deal. Let us pray he knows his
place and will give you no trouble. For
what is an organist in comparison with a
Miss Chloe Crecy? Young men hope
very high nowadays."

"So far as birth goes," said Mrs.
Crecy, "I have no false pride. If a man

is gentleman-like and has an uncle who
is a clerk in the House of Commons—
and that means influence, Mrs. Triptree
—and if he is cousin to a Lady Barrow,
he may always find a friend at 'Randalls'!"

"You surprise me, Mrs. Crecy. I
never heard that Mr. Banish was related
to a lady of title. I knew that he was
well-connected and had a grandfather in
the Navy, but more than this I never
dreamt of!"

"His aunt, my dear, was the Honorable Mrs. Puxter—I heard it all this
morning from Dr. Somers, whose god-
father was her medical man. She died
of dropsy at Brighton, having been tapped
nine times. The world is very small."

"Now I think of Mr. Banish," said
Mrs. Triptree, "he certainly has an air
out of the common. But he's poor, Mrs.
Crecy, very poor, and when a man is
needy, there's no limit to his daring. If

there's sixty thousand pound to be settled on any one, he won't think the less
of them on that account! A word to the
wise is my motto. And Miss Chloe Crecy
need not waste her time with an Honorable's nephew while she has a fortune
worth an Honorable in his own right!"

"La!" said Mrs. Crecy, "Chloe never
thinks of marriage, and as for her papa
and myself we are very humble-minded.
We never push. We gave her a fine
education, to be sure: she speaks French,
sings Italian, and can paint flowers on
wood, china, or common drawing-paper.
I would sooner hear her play than a
musical box, and her dancing is very
much admired. But I never speak of
these things."

"Her looks, Mrs. Crecy, her looks
alone are the talk of Ottley. What a
complexion! But don't let her draw her
stays too tight. She doesn't need it:
her figure is perfection."

"Beauty is but skin-deep, Mrs. Triptree. There's nothing truer than these
old sayings."

"What a delicious scent on your
handkerchief!"

"Made from our own lavender. Let
me send you a bottle. . . . You spoke
in such a way, Mrs. Triptree, that one
would think you had some person in your
mind."

"I never talk for the sake of talking,
Mrs. Crecy. I happened to know that
there is an officer at Lauderston who is
most desirous of making your acquaintance. He's a very fine man indeed, and
own brother to Lord Rendlewick. If you
should invite him here to dinner, I wish
I could be as sure of everything as I am
that my girls would very soon be brides-
maids on a certain happy occasion!"

"You mean the Honorable Charles
Camelot, Mrs. Triptree, who was in
attendance on the General when he

opened the Flower Show at Radley Soham. I remember him well—he talked to Mr. Crecy for a good ten minutes. A little-ish man with long arms and a wart on his left eyebrow. I can well believe that he might be very affable. It may be with him as it is with many—when you say that he's not much to look at, you've said the worst. But how could we ask him to the house, knowing him so little?"

" He is not one to stand on ceremony," said Mrs. Triptree. " Mr. Crecy could call upon him, and then you could write him a nice civil note, saying that you are having a few old friends very quietly to dinner—and so on."

" Then you and the Vicar must fix the date, Mrs. Triptree."

" La! You are far too good. I never once thought that you would want us! Then shall you say Tuesday week?"

" By all means."

"How hot it is getting! Really, it is not the weather for walking."

"Rivers shall drive you home in the pony-chaise, Mrs. Triptree," said Mrs. Crecy, "but we must first have tea."

CHAPTER XII.

Concerning a Goddess of Mortal Speech.

NOW about a fortnight later, Rose and Mrs. Harrowby, her nephew—Sir Harry Blythe, and Colonel Thompson of the —th Lancers were sitting at luncheon in the dining-room at 99 Cavendish Square. The Colonel looked like a plaster cast of Napoleon spoilt in the baking, and his voice sounded as though he had spent his life swallowing crumbs the wrong way. Otherwise he was an amiable gentleman and a brave soldier.

" Our sergeant," he was saying, " picks up the strangest recruits. He aims straight at the love-sick. His latest prey is a factory clerk who was at Eton and Cambridge ! But his papa married a lady with canary-colored hair, lost all his money, and came to smash. This chap is a fine fellow, but melancholy—O Lord! It seems that his sweetheart was already married."

"And he looks melancholy?" said Mrs. Harrowby; "incredible!"

"Scoffer!" said the Colonel. "I can assure you it's a very sad affair. The sergeant heard it from the local draper, and the local draper heard it from his wife. When one woman tells a story to the credit of another woman's virtue—you may depend on its truth."

"I wish to hear no true stories," said Mrs. Harrowby, "or I shall lose my comfortable detestation of life."

"You are as cold in your hatreds as your loves," said the Colonel; "for you establish both on the artificial."

"Fiddle-de-dee!" quoth she. "I adored you for years and I adore you still, yet if you are not a real man, I don't know a hypocrite when I see him! You men always think we are cold if we use words of more than two syllables, and you call us unkind if we profit by your philosophy. Do you remember the day we——"

"All this is very touching," said Sir Harry, who was handsome, bird-eyed, dark, and thirty-eight; "but Mrs. Arden and I have no pretty reminiscences in common, and we should like to hear more about the new recruit."

"I can guess it," said Mrs. Harrowby. "His sweetheart had a husband, and she refused to make bad worse! So this young friend thanked God for her good sense, mistook relief for the heartache, and enlisted. There it is! If a woman wants to keep a man's esteem for ever, let her refuse to run away with him. That is the one thing for which the thankless ruffians never fail to show gratitude!"

"I like to see a woman tender," said

the Baronet, who, if rumor spoke honestly, had deceived a dozen or so in his
time. "I like to see her tender, and, if
possible, sorrowful."

"Of course, Jack Libertine," said his
aunt, "because it is the poor creature in
trouble who will take the greatest risk
for a possible brief happiness! You are
a rogue, sir, and if I ever hear of a wife
in a scrape, I know that Harry Blythe is
to blame for it. Oh, you may look offended and cough—as though honor had
suddenly settled—like a cold—on your
chest! You are a rascal and so is my
dog, Launcelot! Yet I pet you both,
knowing full well, that when I am dead,
he will be ready to pick my bones and
you will sell my skin! And here is Rose
—a sweet, kind soul, who would, I believe,
be fool enough to cry at my funeral, and
I make *her* life a burden and shall not
leave her a shilling. I would never give
money to women, my dear, for of all the

humiliations piled upon our sex, there is none so cruel as to be loved or married for our fortune. The worst husband is to be respected while he pays your bills. It is hard to despise a brute, who, after all, likes you well enough to provide for you. That is why the wives of laboring men are rarely unfaithful. They can feel—even while they are kicked—that they were chosen for themselves—not for their dowries. Let a woman once suspect that she is loved for her money and she will throw her cap over the windmill for the first comer who seems disinterested. We are proud, Thompson; we fall through pride far more than passion."

"Yet," said Rose, timidly, "is it not rather vanity than self-respect which makes a woman so anxious to be wholly dependent on her husband? Even the Homeric Penelope, whom you so often quote, seems to have been very rich."

"That," said Mrs. Harrowby, with a

twinkle in her eye, "is why Odysseus returned to her. He was afraid she would
marry again and take her fortune out of
the family! Homer understood human
nature, my love. Poor Rosie!" she continued; "I never liked Arden, as you
know; but you hadn't a halfpenny piece
when he chose you. It was all for your
face and your good temper, my dear.
Now I was handsomer in my youth than
you would believe, and I had the disposition of a love-bird. I danced like a fairy;
sang like a lark; played the harp, talked
three languages, and God knows what
not! And I had ten thousand a year,
which gave me the refusal of every laggard
in the realm. They all wanted me, my
poor Rosie, they were all so deeply in
debt. Did I marry to please myself?
No, I had—like the rest—not the fear of
God but the fear of the flunky before my
eyes. I chose a husband who would
please my flunkies: my maid, my dress-

maker, my shoemaker and my groom
were all a-gog; my inferiors were all jealous, my equals came, smirking, to the
wedding, and my superiors thought I had
done very well for myself! It was a
glorious day for the footman when I married the Duke of Chale!"

Mrs. Harrowby never wearied of telling
these old stories, nor, during their recital,
did her friends ever miss showing at the
right moments the appropriate signs of
astonishment, admiration, and mirth.
There was often, it must be owned, a
certain vindictiveness in her tone which
would have been called vulgar had she
been a woman of less distinguished birth.
Her constant allusions to her money, her
family name, her marriages, her admirers,
and her exploits would have been intoler-
able but for her good heart and the un-
affected freshness of her manner. She
spoke her mind—and that is a quality
which, if ill-bred, at least can never be

described as commonplace. Sometimes,
in the course of conversation, her own
attention would wander. She would
finish a sentence in her mind, and her
eyes only would betray, by their vivacity
and ever-changing expression, that she
was re-living the drama of her past.

" I was a Duchess," she continued,
"for two very tiresome years. I yawned,
I yapped, I suffered all the tortures of
the respectable. Then my Duke died,
and, for a change, I married a mere Captain in the Guards—the son of a country
squire. But I dropped my title, for, if a
man is good enough to call husband, one
may as well take his name! So I became
plain Mrs. Harrowby, and all my flunkies
were shocked. And my cousin, Sir Aud-
ley de Borne, talked the Prime Minister
blue till he got my Harrowby's uncle at
least knighted—General Sir Frankfort
Harrowby. The greatest duffer in the
Army, too. Poor fellow! At thirty-

three I was left a widow for the second
time and I have lived single ever since,
for the only man I would have looked at
had not the courage to marry me! That
was Ned Banish, Rosie, your father—who
would have been Lord Chancellor had he
but shown more pluck. I have always
played the goddess with men—they
treated me as Odysseus did poor Circe
and Calypso; I told them all my wisdom and gave them fair weather when
they sailed away, without a 'Thank you,'
toward their Penelopes! And what a
minx Penelope was! I never could bear
that woman. Nay, I was always a goddess, my friends. I shed no tears; I
made no scenes; I uttered no reproaches.
But I loved your father, Rosie; he had
the makings of an immortal! Fetch me
his miniature. It is in the fourth drawer
of my writing-table, and the key is on
the third shelf of my wardrobe."

Rose, at this hint, gladly arose from

her chair and hastened from the room
with a very cold acknowledgment to Sir
Harry, who opened the door for her as
she went out.

"Thompson," said Mrs. Harrowby, turning to the Colonel when she had gone,
"you were always a fool. Why must
you have told that story of the new recruit? Rose is the very woman he is
pining for!"

"Good God!" said the Colonel.

"He shows his taste," said Sir Harry;
"she's a seductive creature: subtle-
minded."

"Now, Harry," said Mrs. Harrowby,
turning full upon him, "I'll have none of
your nonsense here. I saw you at lunch
—looking like a shot robin at my meek
Jenny Wren. Have you no moral sense,
sir? Can't I have a poor widow in my
house but you must make love to her
with your eyelashes and pass her the pep-
per as though it were your heart?"

"A widow, aunt?" said he. "I thought her husband was not only alive but mad!"

"Hush!" said she; "he died two days ago. I had a letter from her brother Edward last night, asking me to break the news to her. But I have not told her yet, nor shall I, till our gallant young friend, the love-sick recruit, is well out of England and on his way to India. Edward and he have quarreled, so he will hear nothing from Edward. And Rose dare not say good-bye to him —little fool! She wrote him a note— such a note! God-blessing him and the rest. Ah, Harry, that's a woman in ten thousand. But she wouldn't take you as a gift. She has no opinion of you. She calls you a vain coxcomb—a Dutch doll of a man. And she abhors a rake. You may purr and purr, but you will never make the least impression on her!"

Sir Harry looked as though he had

good reasons for venturing to think
otherwise.

"And when does the virtuous recruit
sail for India?" said he.

"To-morrow," said Mrs. Harrowby.

"Then," said Sir Harry, "I will take
tea with you to-morrow."

"Very well, Tarquin," said she. "Very
well, Lovelace! Nero! Jupiter! Don
Juan! Blue-beard!"

He smiled at the flattering salutation,
bowed to the Colonel, kissed his aunt's
hand, and departed.

"There's a libertine," said she, when
he had gone: "a real villain. Rose is
the only woman who could resist him,
and she is, therefore, the only woman he
should marry! And marry him she shall,
Thompson. I have set my mind upon
it. I will disinherit him if she does not.
I will tell her so, too. She has too much
kindness to see the poor fellow ruined!"

At this moment Rose re-entered.

"I have searched everywhere," said she, "but I cannot find the miniature."

"Dear heart!" said Mrs. Harrowby, with great wonder; "how odd! I could have sworn it was in the fourth drawer. But have some port, my love; you look as pale as milk.   Drink her health, Thompson."

Poor Rose blushed to find herself the object of so much attention. She declined the wine, but the Colonel drank to her happiness with much fervor and a wink at Mrs. Harrowby.

"May your heart be ever *blithe*, Ma'am," said he, with an air of seraphic innocence; "you must cheer up! Better days are coming! 'Tis always darkest before dawn, and every cloud has a silver lining!"

"Thank you," said she. "I am, I hope, very cheerful—very cheerful, indeed! I was never more contented nor so easy in my mind."

And her eyes filled with tears.

"Now, Rosie," said Mrs. Harrowby, "we must drink to this turtle's safe return. He sails to-morrow."

"I know," said Rose, "I have not forgotten. And, Colonel—I have heard from my brother that there's a young man called Arthur Venus—from Ottley—who has enlisted in your regiment. His mother is a widow : he is all she has : and our little maid is his sweetheart. If he should ever get into trouble—and I believe he is rather headstrong—will you remember that there are two women . . . two poor desolate women . . . who love him dearly. But then," she added, "that might be said, no doubt, of all the others. There will, I am sure, be many in trouble to-morrow."

"Many," said the Colonel, refilling his glass; "many. And the men, too, will need all their pluck, I can tell you."

"Crocodile!" said Mrs. Harrowby.

But Rose left the room.

CHAPTER XIII.

In which Mrs. Harrowby is Eloquent.

WHEN Sir Harry called on the morrow, he was filled with disappointment to learn that Mrs. Arden was confined to her room with a headache. Mrs. Harrowby, in a very ill temper, received him, and declared that she herself was not long for this world—so weary was she of its fools and Tom-fools.

"Thompson and his regiment," said she, "left England, as you know, early this morning. Rose brought me my cup of tea as usual at half-past seven, but she came with such a face that I could not drink a spoonful. She had been crying all night, and she looked like a drowned dove."

"Then she has a heart," said Sir Harry, much comforted: "I feared she

was one of those hard women who remember you in their prayers, and, for the
rest of the time, forget you!"

"I could wish," said Mrs. Harrowby,
severely, "that you had met but such admirable creatures!"

"Tell me about Rose," said he.

"She depressed me. 'Rose,' said I, in
the cheerfullest way, 'I have some news
for you. Your husband is dead!' At
this she reeled like a top and fell down in
a swoon. A swoon, sir! I thought
widows swooned in poetry only! And
now she lies on my bed without a word
or a question, staring at the wall."

"Poor girl!" said Sir Harry, kindly,
"she must have been fond of the fellow."

"Once, no doubt, she was," said Mrs.
Harrowby; "and who can tell what may
be passing in her mind? Perhaps she is
thinking of the time when he looked like
a hero, and she is burying that picture."

She glanced at him and thought it a

scandal that such a smooth wretch should not be ruffled by matrimony.

"Rose is not for you," said she; "and I hope you will never be such a fool as to think of marriage."

"I must settle down some day," said he, falling into the trap; "but I am in no hurry."

"You are not to make love to Mrs. Arden."

"My wife must be a woman of the world."

"Rose is no simpleton, but it is difficult to have one's husband in a lunatic asylum and be at once religious, witty, and good-looking!"

"You are flippant," said Sir Harry, somewhat shocked.

"There is no one so serious as a libertine," said Mrs. Harrowby, with a bow.

He flushed.

"I do not wonder," he observed, "that you drove every man away from you."

Mrs. Harrowby admired his pluck for daring to speak so rudely to a sick relation. She could never forget her wealth.

"My dear," said she, "I never drove men away by my chatter—they enjoyed it. But many think it is the chief mission of a devoted wife to tempt her husband to eat more than is good for him. I kept too plain a table, and I never tried to look alluring. I confess to these crimes."

"It is for a husband," said Sir Harry, "to dictate the terms of his existence. I had rather live for ten years in my way than for forty, yours! A wife is neither a trainer nor a keeper——"

"But a slave," said Mrs. Harrowby. "I found that out too late. If I had let my two husbands and my thirty-six wooers go straight to the devil, they would have adored me for ever."

"The charm of Rose lies in the fact,"

said Sir Harry, "that she never makes bitter remarks."

"That is because she has the gift of loving with her eyes shut."

"Do you think that fellow in the country made a deep impression on her?" asked Sir Harry.

"Yes," replied Mrs. Harrowby, "and I will tell you why. So far as I can learn he rarely spoke and they were never alone together. He lived a life of routine, and his history was such a blank that she could make what she pleased of it. She therefore imagined all he might have said, and naturally found his conversation pleasing! For the rest, he was young, handsome, and poor. All this might have led to a story, but virtue with Rose was the first—and not the after—thought."

"Morality," said he, "or virtue—if you prefer to call it so—is a question of good or bad taste. In the circumstances, I

should describe Mrs. Arden's conduct as
showing good taste—nothing more. It
must have been dull, but it was not ridiculous. It may have been feeble, but it
was not sordid."

He looked up with a pleasant smile.

"That is how," he added, "I criticise
life. I want no prude, no hypocrite, no
Magdalene who sins to-day because re-
pentence will become her on the morrow!
I keep my respect for a woman with good
taste."

"Is religion nothing to you, Harry?"

"In Rose's case," he said, drily, "I believe it is genuine : I cannot say more."

"Like many of us," said Mrs. Harrowby, "your vanity is such that when
you hear of any beautiful quality which
you yourself do not possess, you doubt
its existence in any one."

"Don't preach," said her nephew, getting irritable.

She continued :

"You should have developed your heart before your senses—not your senses before your heart. That is why you are so cold."

"Cold?" said he, casting down his eyes.

"Yes," said his aunt, "for there is nothing so cold as passion."

"Really," said he, indignant—"really, my dear aunt——"

"You can go to your club," she replied, "and reconsider all I have been saying. It will bear reflection."

He poured the contents of the cream-jug into his tea-cup, swallowed it, and took his departure.

Then Mrs. Harrowby went to Rose, who still lay on her bed, staring at the wall.

"I suppose," said the old woman, "you will write the news to our mad young friend, the new recruit?"

"No."

" Why not ? "

" How little you know me ! "

"When my Duke died, I telegraphed
at once to my six best friends! However, please yourself. I want you to be
happy—that is all. Harry Blythe sends
you his sympathy."

" Thank him."

" I believe he is fond of you. A good
woman might reform him. He is by no
means the scoundrel he would appear.
In his heart I am convinced he would
like nothing better than a pretty wife,
several children—all resembling himself
—and a few houses. He would ask no
more. And I have never heard him say
a word against marriage. All his opinions
are respectable. Think of him, my love !
Be cheerful. Good heavens ! We take
our joys as though they were trifles, and
act as though melancholy were the only
serious thing in life ! You are still young
—or young enough to regard the Future

as something more lively than a grave-
yard. You must go out and show yourself."

"Impossible!"

"My dear, the dullest of women has
two occasions when she can command all
eyes—at her own wedding and at her
husband's funeral."

"Am I a mountebank?"

"No," said Mrs. Harrowby; "you are
the fool who risks her neck to jump
through a paper hoop! You ride too
high a horse."

"What have I done?" cried Rose.

"When my father lost his temper,"
continued Mrs. Harrowby, "he always
killed two dogs and kicked the footman
lame. I have his spirit!"

"If I have offended you," said Rose,
"speak out!"

"You enjoy suffering," said Mrs. Harrowby; "you nurse your misery. If I
could but persuade you that marriage is

a martyrdom, you would marry again to-morrow. I am above such silly deceptions. If you accepted Harry Blythe you would be happy—I repeat it, happy!"

Rose sat up and smoothed back her disordered hair.

"What do you mean?" said she.

"You could get him," observed Mrs. Harrowby; "play your cards well and you can be Lady Blythe—all, merely for your face and your irritating manner. I have set my heart upon it. I will see one love-match before I die, please God."

"My dear friend," said Rose, quietly, "you talk like a woman in a dream."

"I will give dinner-parties; I will buy you fine gowns," said Mrs. Harrowby; "you shall appear at every advantage. And if he has the sense to marry you, I will leave him every penny of my money."

"I don't want him," said Rose.

"No," said Mrs. Harrowby, "you prefer Robsart. You will sacrifice all things for a man who would write on your tombstone, '*Here lies some one whose name I have forgotten!*' Your father all over again!"

Rose dissolved into tears, and fell back weeping on her pillow.

"Have I ever seen such weakness?" said Mrs. Harrowby. "Have I ever known of such folly? Was there ever so cruel—so pitiless a woman? Poor Harry Blythe just waits for your word to become a new creature. You have the chance to save a noble soul—yet you refuse it. You will watch him seek out—in desperation—some fawning Delilah; you will permit him to be disinherited; you will see a brilliant career played away in country houses, obscure hotels, and inglorious boudoirs! An outrage!"

"It is impossible," said Rose, "that he could have the smallest interest in me.

We have not exchanged a dozen words in confidence."

"You have made him timid—what better proof could you ask of his affection?"

"I am neither beautiful nor clever," continued Rose; "I am poor and ordinary. What could he see in me?"

"Now I think of it," observed Mrs. Harrowby, with an air of abstraction, "that wicked Delilah but cut off Samson's hair. The pious Jael, however, cut off her lover's head!* You good creatures are so severe. Why analyze Blythe's feelings? You attract him—you tempt him to reform! Is not that sufficient?"

Rose dried her eyes, and walked from the bed to the dressing-table.

"Look at me!" she said: "I am faded and heart-broken. What man would remember me?"

She was thinking of Robsart.

* *Mrs. Harrowby had no doubt read Balzac.*

"An inexperienced man," said Mrs. Harrowby, following her mind, "would forget you at once—because he would not have the sense to know that you were rare. But you are foolish to indulge in these cryings and frettings. Penelope would have looked a hag on her husband's return if the goddess had not given her a second youth. And there are no more goddesses! So think of your complexion. No grief is worth a wrinkle. Did you ever see a finer skin than mine?"

"Never."

" It is the result of cream and philosophy : cream during sleep and philosophy all day !"

A little pink gaiety budded in Rose's pale cheeks.

"You are wonderful," said she: "you are the one woman in the world—you can love and be wise!"

"What do you know of love?" asked Mrs. Harrowby.

"Not much," she said, hastily; "not much."

"That's a lie."

"I had affection for my husband—and I have had . . . a friendship!"

"The friendship made more impression than the husband?"

"I was older . . ."

"Describe Robsart again! Show me his picture!"

"I have none."

Mrs. Harrowby looked grave. Were matters so serious? "What?" said she; "you dare not keep his photograph?"

"I *need* not," said Rose.

"His face is always before you?"

"Always," said Rose, quietly.

This candor was unexpected. Had Rose already caught the audacity born of freedom?

"He is a pauper," said Mrs. Harrowby, after a long pause.

"He is a king!"

"He could not support you!"

"I worship him."

"This," said Mrs. Harrowby, "is un-
seemly . . . What will you live on?
Virtue by itself makes a thin diet."

"We shall never marry."

"Blythe is not a man who would permit his wife to be a saint-tamer!"

"What do you think I meant?"

"What most women mean, when they
speak of kings whom they cannot marry,
and mere friends—whom they worship!
You will eat your breakfast bacon with
my poor Harry, and read poetry with
Robsart!"

This suggestion was so false that Rose
laughed aloud.

"A clerk," continued Mrs. Harrowby,
"is a salaried hypocrite. He is a grain
of brickdust in the great pyramids of
middle-class stupidity! Good God!
You know these things as well as I do!
What did you see in the man?"

"A soul," said Rose.

"Then he *did* ask you to run away with him?" said Mrs. Harrowby, at once.

"Never."

"Invertebrate," murmured the older woman. "I like my souls embodied!"

"He was poor," said Rose, hotly; "he had nothing to offer. How was it possible to run away?"

"Then you yourself wondered at his weakness?"

"Not at all."

"Why have you such ready—and so many—excuses for him? One would have answered!"

Rose blushed.

"I should have refused . . ." she stammered ". . . in any case."

"I could never forgive a man," said Mrs. Harrowby, "who gave me no opportunity to show my superior virtue. He was a very dull dog, my dear—a very dull dog. If it were not for the tempters like Harry Blythe, we should never know a chaste woman from a gallant. We owe them much. How could I feel the paragon of wifely honor if some twelve libertines had not plotted my downfall?"

She could see her beauty—placid, pale, ethereal—in the mirror. And she smiled with the understanding innocence one might suppose lit up the face of the infant Pallas Athene—had that goddess, let it be said, ever been an infant.

"Forget the fellow," she continued; "forget that episode of gooseberry wine and honeysuckle porches! At twenty we long for love; at five-and-twenty we look for companionship; at five-and-thirty we are more anxious for a comfortable environment. Blythe can give you a home and a position—those things abide. Mourn in white garments, dear Rose; dry your tears with lace! Most of our fine sentiments come from the stomach—remember that always. The soul is horridly cold-blooded!"

Then she went into the oratory which led off from her bedroom.

CHAPTER XIV.

A Lady Talks Sense and Comedy Looks Tearful.

OTTLEY, about this time, was flaming with scarlet posters which announced a Liberal Fête to be opened the following afternoon by

The Hon CHARLES BELLEBOROUGH, M. P.,

in the grounds of " Randalls."

Edward received a note from Mrs. Crecy inviting him to luncheon "before the ceremony" at half-past one.

"Why is it," he asked himself, " that we cannot gaze with due appreciation on a hero till we have gorged our stomachs with *made dishes ?* "

To Mr. Lawrence and Mr. Sledges,

however, he spoke like a good citizen of
the coming Fête. Such things brought
all classes of society together; they
amused the young people; helped the
Liberal Cause, which, after all, charlatan-
ism, clap-trap and time-serving apart, was
a sound one. Read history: forget plat-
forms! Take the solid result—not the
ephemeral methods of obtaining it. If
hypocrisy succeeded—it proved that the
deceived public clung to ideals. When
cant was found necessary, it meant that
voters at least were sincere. He had, for
some reason, lost all his cynicism, and if
he barked now—it was only at the moon
for not shining all day.

When, on the morrow, he was ushered
into Mrs. Crecy's drawing-room, Chloe
and a young man were sitting by the
fireplace, and, as Edward entered, the
girl was laughing with affected joyous-
ness at her visitor's remarks. She addressed him as Captain Camelot.

Belleborough, the Member for Ottley,
who stood listening to Mr. Crecy's views
on Colonial Industries, was a stern man
who commanded an immense amount of
respect and was regarded with unwilling
awe. He had neither enemies nor friends ;
men agreed with him or disagreed with
him, and, while his supporters found him
blameless, his opponents thought him
nothing worse than dull. His conversation that day at luncheon was appropriate and unmemorable. The guests present
were, with the exceptions of Edward and
the Captain, Crecy's own relatives who
were staying at " Randalls " for the occasion. It was the brewer's wish to give
the entertainment the air of a family
party, and, if trembling silence in the
women, cautious drinking among the
men, brand-new dresses on the one, and
settled melancholy in the other, can be
said to indicate the careless ease of a
domestic circle, Charles Belleborough

and his daughter, who accompanied him, had certainly every reason to believe that they were taken to the very heart of their host's home-life. When the meal was ended, the ladies adjourned to the drawing-room, the gentlemen strolled laboriously after them, and the servants rearranged the table for dinner, in order that the public, now promenading outside the windows, might enjoy the spectacle of Crecy's plate, crockery, table-linen, and cut-glass set out in the most correct manner.

The Town Band played martial, and the Volunteer Band amorous airs, in turn; some school children sang (while Belleborough concealed but unsuccessfully his patriotic emotions) "Rule, Britannia." Crecy pressed him reverently on the arm and they passed out, in procession, to the grounds, where, in a pink tent set apart for the fashion and first families of Ottley, he took a red velvet chair on a

little platform and heard himself intro-
duced as the coming glory of his country
and its present mainstay. Amy, his
daughter, sat at his right and showed no
signs of hearing the loud comments of
the Ottley gentlewomen on the subject
of her hat, her gown, and her general appearance. A few condemned, but more
approved, the simplicity of her attire,
which made no lady present feel herself
dowdy and gave most of them a pleasant
sense of possessing the taste, were they
in her position, to produce a far more im-
posing effect. As her garments did not,
therefore, excite any painful or envious
comparisons, but on the contrary, those
which were most solacing and charitable,
the audience were better able to confine
their attention to Belleborough's well-de-
livered speech.

Belleborough had made his name for
moral orthodoxy, and, although there are
always a certain number of persons who

find it difficult to believe that any one
should ever be in earnest except when he
attacks received opinion, the Member for
Ottley had escaped, in an age of general
scepticism, the charge of hypocrisy. He
meant what he said. If his eloquence
sounded, on some occasions, high-flown,
it was because the times were easy-going,
not because his maxims were untried.

The Fête was declared a national dem-
onstration : great was the applause and
greater the embarrassment of those who
had come expecting to be amused.
The local photographer applied his cam-
era to the group; Mr. Crecy informed
the audience that there were Indian jug-
glers and other attractions without, and
the meeting dispersed.

Crecy drove the Belleboroughs to the
railway station, and, after their departure,
an easier merriment settled on the house-
party. Mrs. Crecy suggested that Chloe
should sing—at which point Edward

realized, to his chagrin, that he had been invited solely for the honor of playing the heiress's accompaniment. The Captain's ravished demeanor during her song filled the organist with the worst apprehensions; he recognized the Wooer in his attitude, and the Son-in-law in Mrs. Crecy's smile. He found it impossible to remain in their society, and, making an abrupt adieu, he hastened from the house.

Now about nine o'clock that same evening, Miss Chloe walked toward the cottage of Mrs. Venus, and she carried on her arm a basket of dainties for that deserted woman. Mrs. Venus lived some two hundred yards from the gate of Wrestle's Farm, and it so happened that Edward, as Miss Chloe passed, stood there waiting—perhaps for the carrier.

"What a surprise!" exclaimed Miss Crecy, in tones of great astonishment.

"I feel none," replied Edward, grimly.

"I am so distressed," said she, "about poor Mrs. Venus."

"Your sympathies," he said, with a mocking smile, "are wide."

She looked away.

"Don't be cruel," she whimpered.

"Oh, Chloe!"

He clenched his hands and grew pale.

"Allow me," he said, with a false air of self-possession, "to take that basket!"

She gave it up and put back her veil. She needed all her beauty at that moment.

"Can I disobey my parents?" she asked. "Shall I break my mother's heart?"

"You are so clever," said Edward, still bitter, "that in any case you will certainly come to grief. For it takes a born fool to drive a good bargain with life."

"You never give a direct answer," said Chloe; "you are always in the clouds!"

"I have been walking on earth, at all

events, for the last fortnight! . . . Do
you intend to marry that man?"

"Give me time to refuse him!"

"You are considering the question?
Good God!"

"I will not accept his offer—against
your wish. Nor can I marry you—
against my father's. I will remain as I
am always . . . if you think . . . a solitary, unloved existence would suit me!"

She sighed, drew off her gloves, and laid
a cool palm on Edward's trembling arm.

"We could always be great friends,"
said she.

"Never."

"If you are a genius—I am not sure
that you ought to marry—even me!"

"You did not talk in this strain," said
Edward, "when we first met!"

"Your fascination overruled my reason."

"Oh," he cried, breaking away from
her touch, "how happy we were!"

"But so unusual," said Chloe, half shocked. Beer and the conventions had been poured out so liberally on her soul that Romance could but float there like a water-lily on an unmoving pool.

"I always knew," she continued, "that it could lead to nothing. You see, Edward, I am an only child. If I had sisters—brothers—who could make brilliant matches, I might permit myself an experiment. But all my father's hopes are fixed on me. I dare not fail him. I love you—believe me, I love you very dearly. If you had any sort of position to offer me—I would marry you!"

"That will do," said he; "no more! Take the Captain!"

She wept.

"One must be reasonable," she said; "one cannot re-make the world."

"Every genius that is born," he exclaimed, "gives the world a new turn! You are servile."

"I never claimed to be a genius," said she; "I merely wish to do my duty."

"The duty of a beautiful woman," he answered, "is to inspire hearts—not to preach sordid maxims. *If I had any sort of position to offer you—you would take me!* Merciful heavens! Am I a man? You don't want a husband, but some creature who will provide you with a visiting list!"

"Do I care what you are?" cried Chloe; "I know your gifts! But my father is practical: it is on his account, not mine, that I wish you had worldly success."

"Has Camelot proposed to you?"

"Not yet."

"Oh, Chloe," murmured the unhappy young man, "it is not for me to say that he loves you solely for your money. I can well believe that he loves you for yourself. You are so pretty."

They had now reached the cottage of

Mrs. Venus, but the windows were dark,
and the widow had evidently gone to
bed.

"I can come again in the morning,"
said Chloe, and she sat down on a pile of
stones by the road. Edward, standing
by her side, looked upon her, with aching
temples. In all true love-stories there is
always some inequality of heart or fortune which, sooner or later, tempts one
soul to despair, and the other to false
pride. Chloe had reached the moment
of discontent.

"What would your father call a *position*?" said Edward.

"Parliament," said Chloe, briefly; "the
Army; the Diplomatic Service. He
doesn't think so much of the Bar and the
Church."

"Give me a little time, then," said he;
"I have some friends who might . . . I
will never again think of music . . . I
will go to London to-morrow . . . I can

be worldly . . . I can get a Secretary-
ship . . . give me time."

"How long?" said the maiden.

"Two or three days. . . . You have
reason on your side, dearest. . . . A
country organist! A choir-master! . . .
What presumption on my part. . . .
What is Art compared with Life? A
dead letter. Let me live first. I will
make a large income. How much do
you want? I would take nothing from
your father—not a penny."

"Could you make four thousand a
year?"

"Easily!" said the genius.

She shook her head.

"Mr. Belleborough," said she, "gives
his secretary two pounds a week!"

This was discouraging.

"Never mind," said Edward, getting
pale; "I have schemes."

"What sort of schemes?" asked Chloe.

" Why dissipate my energy in talking

about them?" said the youth; "give
me time—that is all I ask."

"Whatever happens," she said, "you
know one thing—I love you."

"Angel!"

"No," she said, serenely, "I am not an
angel. I do not wish to be considered
one. I am a sensible girl who has permitted herself to behave rather foolishly!
But I am devoted to you, dear Edward,
and neither time nor distance can lessen
my affection for you."

She spoke primly. Has she a heart?
thought Edward. He dived into her
eyes with his own blindfolded—and felt
no chill.

"Enigma!" he said.

Chloe took his hand, and pressed it to
her cheek.

"We are talking sense," she said, softly,
"you must remember that we are talking
sense. It isn't so pleasant as . . . the
other!"

"What other?"

"Non-sense, dearest."

"Our long walks . . . our talks . . . our sympathy, were those nonsense?" cried Edward; "did you not say that our souls were predestined for each other?"

"Of course," she answered; "our *souls* got on extraordinarily well. But if you remember, I never once said that we ought to be engaged! To begin with, I do not approve of long engagements!"

"Herb-Moons!" said Edward, to himself, "Herb-Moons!"

"You are so odd," said Chloe; "you use such strange expressions. Poetry— after tea—at a garden-party is appropriate enough, because the weather is usually fine and one is in the humor to say things that sound well!"

"High-minded small talk!" said Edward, with a cutting smile. "We have met many times, however, since that gar-

den-party—in rain and at twilight: in
the cemetery and by the old barn! I
thought you were in earnest always."

"I was," she replied—"I was in earnest. And I am in earnest now. But
may I never change my mood? The
past was all Spring: it is time to be serious and Autumnal!"

Edward grasped at her excuse.

"No doubt," said he, "delicious, in-
consistent April is as much in earnest as
grave November! She lasts as long!
she rules the earth her thirty days!"

Miss Crecy smiled wearily. She could
endure Edward's fantastic utterances so
long only as they were addressed to her
own eyes. *Delicious April* sounded too
much like some other woman to be a
pleasing figure of speech.

"There is a time," said she, "when one
must be business-like. People fall in love,
marry, and postpone the sober facts of
life for discussion—till after the wedding-

journey! And because the facts are sober and have to be discussed seriously, they are called a disillusion! How much better it is to plunge into business matters first and *know where you are*—before you start on your honeymoon! I should not love a man less because I thought his means insufficient to marry on, nor should I love him more because the settlements were wholly satisfactory. I am very sane, Edward."

"You are, indeed," he replied.

"You see," she continued, in calm tones, "your pride is so great that it would break your heart to be absolutely dependent on my fortune. I feel this strongly. On the other hand, I have not the courage to forego my fortune and live on what you could earn for me. It would preserve your self-respect at the cost of my health. And what is worse than an invalid wife? I have been reading about geniuses lately. They do not answer."

"When you talk like that," he cried,
"I could almost hate you!"

"Men always detest plain-speaking,"
she said.

"If you were not beautiful, you would
be inexcusable!"

"I am determined to use my brains,"
she replied; "and surely, when I speak
so reasonably about money matters, you
can believe me, when I add in the same
breath that you are the one being in the
world I love! If I do not talk in the
usual false strain, it is not because I rate
sentiment too low, but because I rate it
before all things!"

"It cannot be bought," said Edward,
"it can only be lost! In this conversation we have lost it for ever!"

Chloe looked at him in amazement.
Why could he not be sane? why this un-
willingness to face life as a house-holder?
She rose from the heap of stones and
stood up beside him.

"Edward," said she, "one of us, of course, must be wrong. But if I am too worldly, you are too rash."

She put her arms around his neck with that deliberate impetuosity which made her recklessness as cold as her common sense.

"I love you, dear," she said, "and I will wait . . . a few days. Good-night. You must leave me now because I hear the ponies."

She had ordered the groom to call for her with the chaise at Mrs. Venus's cottage.

Edward kissed her miserably and stole away as the carriage loomed in the distance. His heart was writhing. These secret meetings and stealings away filled him with self-contempt. He crept home to fling his frantic mood at Heaven and his uneasy body on a bed. He cursed his weakness; blamed the whole system of creation; thought of Chloe's eyes;

remembered the fragrance of her face ;
brooded on ways of suicide.

It is an orthodox doctrine—and a use-
ful—that for every scene of life there are
invisible spectators—an audience of good
and evil spirits. We may believe, therefore, that the air during the walk to Mrs.
Venus's cottage, and now in Edward's
room, was thick with sulphur and myrrh,
and the space crowded with hoofs and
wings. We may go even further and
presume that on this occasion it was un-
usually dense, for, no doubt, the word
had gone round among the ministers of
grace and the agents of destruction that
two young people in love were about to
meet, in the common unhappy circumstances, and about to talk in the usual
lunatic strain. Love, however, has no
sameness for the immortals : it is their
current coin ; and just as the sober among
us reserve our best attention for the
daily money-market and the seventh-

daily sermon on Unworldliness—our little angels and our little devils look eagerly at the Love-Mart. For there are the beginnings of all things—spiritual and earthy.

While Edward was tossing on his bed, the angels looked at the fiends. The leader of the evil ones—who was gentlemanlike, and carried a volume of poetry behind his big ear—observed: "He shows great inexperience. One of you might have prompted him. There is gross carelessness somewhere."

"This is Comedy's interference," said his colleague on the right; "she is a nuisance."

He shot a glance at the Muse who sat opposite. She had in her eyes eternal tears which never fell. She was too nearly human to be completely satisfied with her work.

"I have great respect for your power, Comedy," said the first fiend, "but you

lack logic. And you will not understand
that the passions are serious. Here to-
day was an opportunity wasted. Every
time you step into a love-scene, we either
find virtue triumphant or common sense
made to sound absurd! You inspire
plain, indelicate language, and are as
truthful as our vulgar friend—the Record-
ing Angel!"

Then his followers clattered away, plot-
ting malice and singing pretty songs
about life. But Comedy and the good
spirits remained, looking anxious.

CHAPTER XV.

The Question of Edward's Soul.

THE next afternoon, Rose was on her knees in the drawing-room at Cavendish Square, darning a small rent in the old brocade of a Louis Seize chair, when the door was suddenly thrown open and Edward Banish announced.

"Edward!" she exclaimed: "I hardly knew you without your beard! What has brought you to London?"

"Many things," said he, sitting down. "I have much on my mind. You are looking well and seem in comfortable surroundings. Did Robsart come here before he left?"

"No," said she, getting pale; "I wrote him good-bye, but I did not see him. Tell me about yourself."

He hesitated.

" I am in danger," he said, at last, " of growing cynical. I doubt everything and everyone."

" That means that you can no longer believe in yourself ! " said his sister, gravely.

"Oh, I was sincere enough," he groaned.

He blurted out his story ; the sudden loves of Chloe and himself ; their clandestine meetings ; the arrival on the scene of Lord Rendlewick's brother ; the heiress's changed tone ; their last interview. It was a breathless tragi-comic history.

" I feel it ! " he exclaimed, at the end : " it is a genuine emotion. This is not a question of liver or nerves or idleness. It has gone to my heart. I am broken ! I am destroyed ! "

" Poor child ! " said Rose ; " poor boy ! "

" I love her," he said, wofully ; " my life was at her feet. And yet she can talk like a solicitor ! "

"If it has made you bitter, it was not love," said Rose.

"I must say what I think. She has no soul! She is all ambition—petty ambition. I despise her."

His pale countenance belied this sentiment.

Rose, in spite of her grief at the poor fellow's disappointment, felt a quiet, motherly satisfaction in the thought that this experience was, after all, the best thing that could befall him. Love had touched his life. It could never now be fruitless.

"She has made me desperate," he continued: "I have decided to get on in the world! I would sell my soul if I could find the devil. But he seems to get as many as he wants now—for nothing!"

"What are your plans?" asked Rose, quietly; "at present they seem mostly dust and sulphur!"

"I thought of Mrs. Harrowby," said

Edward; "she has influence. I have always been too proud to ask her help, but now I am prepared to swallow anything!"

"Yet you tell me," said Rose, "that you are in love! Dear Edward, if you are false to your ideals, life, in turn, will be false to you."

"What are the Ideals?" he asked, savagely; "will they keep a decent roof over my head? will they give me the wife I want? will they pay for her gowns and my ambition? will they earn me so much as one night's easy sleep? I am sick of swearing by phantoms."

Rose disregarded his petulance. She had suffered too much to be astonished at despair.

"I cannot feel," she said, "that Chloe Crecy has behaved so cruelly as you imagine. She has not accepted this other man—she merely contemplates him; and that may mean little! But you could not expect her to marry you in your present circumstances. Her parents would certainly—perhaps rightly—disapprove of such a step."

"I see! I understand!" he exclaimed, "all good women are mercenary."

"All good women are sane."

"Sane?" he repeated, "that is Chloe's eternal word."

"Then she will wait for you."

"Wait for me? How long does that mean? Why can't people marry while they love each other? When I have moiled and toiled all the enthusiasm out of my life, when I shall have schooled myself to *postpone* my bride for some ten years—I shall be in precisely the state of mind to remain a bachelor!"

"If that is so," said Rose, "how fortunate for both of you that you cannot bind yourselves for eternity on the impulse of this mood!"

"I have not your slow blood," said

Edward. Then he seemed to remember her changed circumstances.

"I meant to write to you," he began, awkwardly, "about Arden. But I could find nothing to say. It was too painful. I hate pain."

"So do I," said Rose, simply.

"He's dead, and you have your life before you. The whole trouble has ended much better than I could have hoped. Let us talk no more about it. . . . You asked to know my plans. Somebody must want a secretary . . . . I think of Parliament. . . . After all, Father was destined for a great public career. . . . He made his mark. . . . Had he lived two years longer he would have been Solicitor-General. Every one says so. Why not leave Art and Music to foreigners? Vaguely . . . I felt as much . . . even at Cambridge. Chloe may be right—you yourself grant as much. I shall appeal to Mrs. Harrowby. She wanted to help Father; she can help me. They say I grow more like him every day."

"That is true," said Rose; "the resemblance is astounding."

She was troubled at the thought of Mrs. Harrowby's possible influence on Edward. Would he not take her worldliness too seriously? Would he understand that her vulgarity came rather from egoism than coarse feelings?

At that moment, however, Mrs. Harrowby entered. As she caught sight of Edward, she tottered and must have fallen if Rose had not rushed forward to support her.

"Banish," she said, faintly; "Banish all over again!" and she burst into tears —the slow, spare tears of the aged.

The young man smiled sympathy and admiration. His figure was his father's; his clothes were shabby. Mrs. Harrowby, observing them, resolved, on

the spot, to allow him a thousand a
year.

"I have not seen you, my boy," said
she, "since you were a child of three!
In those days you resembled your
mother. I never admired her. But you
have grown a handsome fellow."

He kissed her hand. His father had
certainly loved this lady, but he had
lacked the courage to face her arrogance.
Now that she was old and weak, however,
it was hard to believe that she had ever
been too terrible to woo in earnest.

"Why are you in London?" she
asked; "you look melancholy."

He blushed.

"A love affair?" said she.

He sighed.

"Tell your story," said Rose.

He told it—let it be known, too, honestly. At its close he looked straight at
Mrs. Harrowby.

"I thought of you at once," he observed; "I felt sure you would help me."

"In what way?" said the old woman.

"By your influence."

"I need all my political influence for my nephew, Harry Blythe. I can do nothing for you in that direction."

This was a blow. He lost his color. But Mrs. Harrowby smiled pleasantly.

"Stick to your Music," said she; "remain a genius! But give up that girl."

"I cannot."

"You really want to marry her?"

He bowed his head.

"Would you take her without a farthing?"

"Gladly."

She paused; then turned to Rose.

"I believe," said she, "that the boy means it. He is absurd, but I like him."

"He is in too great a hurry," said Rose, smiling sadly. "Love is nothing if not patient."

"I abhor a patient lover," said Mrs. Harrowby.

Edward felt encouraged and shot a defiant glance at his painful sister.

"*Hang up philosophy*," he sighed, "*unless philosophy can make a Juliet!*"

Mrs. Harrowby clapped her hands.

"Hang up philosophy," said Rose, drily, "and you will end by hanging yourself."

"Listen!" observed Mrs. Harrowby, "listen! my dove begins to talk like an owl. What has come over you, Rose?"

"I feel that you are advising Edward badly," she replied, with rising color: "I know his disposition. A month ago he hated all women and thought marriage odious. Now he is dying for a girl he has seen a dozen times, and swears he cannot exist without a wife! I distrust these violent changes. These young people who quote *Romeo and Juliet* remember the Ballroom and the Balcony, but they are by no means prepared to follow their heroic patterns to the tomb."

"Rose," said Mrs. Harrowby, "has spent her life studying last acts!"

"I like to know the end of a story," said Rose; "the end is everything!"

"But the beginning is important, too," said Mrs. Harrowby with a certain peevishness; "this poor boy is merely anxious to begin!"

"Is he working?" asked Rose.

"How can I work," said the young man, angrily, "with a mind distraught?"

"To be sure," said Mrs. Harrowby, "how can he?"

"My life is in disorder," he continued; "there is a calculating calm . . . a deliberate endurance about Rose which is—to me—as inexplicable as it is annoying!"

Both women laughed—as most women do when patience is mistaken for want of feeling.

"Does your Chloe believe in your

genius?" asked Mrs. Harrowby, drying
her eyes.

"She would like it more generally
recognized," said Edward, with some
bitterness.

"Every girl likes to see her choice
justified," replied Mrs. Harrowby; "that
is natural enough."

"But," said Rose, "she cannot expect
him to start where other men—after
years of suffering, endeavor, and hard
work—are leaving off."

In spite of her apparent severity, her
heart was on Edward's side. She would
have liked—even against her own better
judgment—a generous recklessness on
Chloe Crecy's part. There is always
something irresistibly touching—if dam-
nable—about an indiscreet marriage. One
condemns the folly but adores the faith
of young, unquestioning passion. It will
toss away the great, grim, heavy world as
though it were an air-ball!

"Dear," said Rose, in a softer tone, "this is your Test. You must bear it. If you are so ready to give up your music—which you have again and again assured me is all that you live for—you will be as willing, later on, to sacrifice Chloe for some one or something else which may seem, for an instant, more desirable. Music is, unquestionably, your gift. Be grateful for it. Public life is often demoralizing: a purely domestic life may make one narrow-minded: an artistic life is perhaps the noblest. Be-cause—whether its emotions endure or perish—*while* they endure they are at least inspiring. And the moment they cease to be inspiring, you cease to be an artist!"

Mrs. Harrowby opened her eyes.

"Our little Rosie," said she, "is be-ginning to show her spirit. That's good advice, Edward: I would never have given it myself; but I know it's good.

Be patient, and grateful, and industrious,
and if Chloe won't love you, God will!"

"But if Chloe doesn't love you,"
added Rose, smiling, "you must, nevertheless, always love Chloe."

"That's tame!" said Mrs. Harrowby.

"That's true love," said Rose.

"Pshaw!" exclaimed the older woman,
with swimming eyes. Her heart was on
the rack, because of Edward's resemblance to his father.

"There is no reason," she said, "why
the boy should bury himself at Ottley.
We must find him work in London.
Does he teach? does he compose? does he
play the organ well enough for a rich parish? could he write a few pretty songs?"

"No," said he, "but I have published
one act of a tragic opera."

"Play it," said Mrs. Harrowby, pointing amiably to the piano; "I don't want
to hear the whole thing—I can judge by
the tenor's first solo!"

He seated himself at the piano and sang melodiously a thrilling air. Mrs. Harrowby was delighted.

"I can imagine the orchestra," she exclaimed, "wild, trembling violins, and now and then the flute! Ravishing! And introduce a harp when the words are Platonic! Delicious! My dear Rose, he is brilliant!"

She kept the young man at the piano for the next two hours; she promised to lead all London to his feet; she talked of glory and fame till he saw—in a prophetic vision—his own monument in Westminster Abbey. And his eyes grew moist at the statuesque idea. The laurel on some brows soon turns into the Lotus flower. Edward had too indolent a nature to support the responsibility of an early success.

"I will give a party," said Mrs. Harrowby. "I will ask all the great amateurs to meet you—Lady Harrian, and

Gerald Arbour, and Mrs. Van Cuyp—
every one. You shall be a celebrity!
Tell your Chloe that!"

"How easy it sounds," said Rose, "all
fame and no work. No, dear Edward,
you must go abroad, live very simply,
and study!"

"You expect a man to think as though
he had no body," said Edward, "and to
act as though he had no soul! Mrs.
Harrowby understands me—you don't!
I need encouragement, sympathy . . ."

"And applause," added Mrs. Harrowby.

"Appreciation," he suggested, as a
meeker word.

"To be sure," said the older lady;
"he is not at all the sort of genius for
six devoted friends and a chimney corner! Rose is so austere!"

Poor Rose reproached herself for being
harsh. Why should she always be forced
to act and speak in direct opposition to
her indulgent—all too indulgent—in-

stincts? How much pleasanter it would
have been to sit there, in silence, gra-
ciously inactive while Edward stained
his spirit with degrading hopes! Philosophy is an amusement to those who feel
nothing, and death to those who feel too
much. Rose had always felt too keenly,
and the constant war of reason against
her passionate ease-loving nature made
her, she thought, often seem heartless
when she was merely heart-broken.

" I know," she said, with a forced smile,
"that I have a fatal passion for excel-
lence in others! "

"You are a dear creature," exclaimed
Mrs. Harrowby, in a great gust of affection ; "you are quite right and I am
quite wrong, and if Edward has a grain of
common sense he will say the same! "

The young man was bewildered. He
began to comprehend his father's reluc-
tance to become one flesh with a being so
various as Paulina Harrowby. There
was no security in her presence.

"Then what do you want me to do?"
he exclaimed.

"Work!" said both women in a
breath.

" And Chloe? " said he, " what about
Chloe?"

" Be faithful," said Rose.

" Look about you!" advised Mrs.
Harrowby: "she may be charming, but
she is not helpless enough to please me.
I think a woman should be helpless.
It moves a man's heroic instinct. Al-
ways be heroic, Edward."

" I will," he said, yawning from sheer
exhaustion.

" But the best of all, dear boy, is to
avoid women altogether," she continued.
" The strong man thinks of other
things!"

He rose from the piano-stool, and, too
weary to be otherwise than natural,
dropped himself, as it were, on the easiest
chair in the room.

"Then I am to return to Ottley," said he, " and tell Chloe that—that——"

" That you would be most false to her by being false to your work," said Rose. " Be strong, Edward."

The tired boy burst into tears. God, the angels, and women know that even the hardest of men cannot escape the necessity of weeping. And Edward was not hard : no musician could be.

"Am I to see her . . . every day," said he, " with that man? What do you think I am made of? If I had my way I would shoot him! Oh, I understand jealousy ! I understand everything now —the Seventh Commandment above all others! I regard her as my wife. I cannot help it. When I saw her that day at ' Randalls,' I knew her at a glance. She was to be the woman of my life. If other men are less impressionable—I am sorry for them! I had rather love one creature too well than too many—too little! I have no desire to be in the fashion."

"My brother speaks," thought Rose, proudly; "he is at last—himself!"

He stood up. The tears had carried away the last remnant of his indecision.

"You can ask me to look on," he said, "and work,—*work* while the woman I love marries another man! My father did that, and the general opinion condemned him. He was thought far too generous!"

"People are always called weak," said Rose, "when they do not act for their own advantage."

"And rightly," he exclaimed, "rightly! I hope I may never mistake cowardice for resignation. I shall make the effort. I shall appeal to Chloe once more. She has sworn that she loves me. And, with all her faults, I believe that she spoke the truth. On the whole, I regard jealousy as a noble passion. Is it not a divine attribute? Your own is your own. Chloe is mine—for richer or poorer. If she is false to me, let the consequences fall upon her own head! I may in time become philosophical on the subject, but my moment for philosophy has not yet come. I will be a man first and a saint later!"

His voice broke. Mrs. Harrowby held out her hand to him.

"Tell all this to Chloe," said she; "frighten her! treat her with contempt! Teach her to regard you with a grovelling respect—and she will follow you proudly, into cheap lodgings at Ealing! I know women. They adore great emotions; they detest equanimity! But keep the emotions *great :* never let them dwindle to the poodle dog's ki-yi!"

Mrs. Harrowby's language was ever vigorous. Her words were like bread soaked in vinegar. She often spoke wisdom, yet she sauced her counsel with such bitterness that few could swallow it.

"Cheap lodgings!" repeated Edward, aghast. "I had forgotten that side of the question!"

"It is the whole question!" said Mrs. Harrowby. "It will be thought out under the summer moon and acted in a little back room, with a smoking chimney, smuts in the air, hashed mutton on the table, and Chloe shivering by the coal-scuttle in an old opera cloak! I have seen such pictures—Enthusiasm at home!"

"Impossible," said Rose, "impossible! Enthusiasm never yet sat shivering by a smoking chimney!"

Mrs. Harrowby tittered.

"Rose is so active," said she; "she would coax the coals, cut the mutton into stars, cast lavender water in the air, and make her opera cloak into a window curtain! But she isn't usual."

"Go back to Ottley," whispered Rose to her brother, "and ask Chloe if she can be patient."

This advice seemed good—so far as it went. He kissed his sister good-bye. Mrs. Harrowby patted him on the shoulder. He went forth realizing that the greater part of life has to be lived alone, and wondering why the struggle for companionship should be made to seem worth while. Mrs. Harrowby, on the other hand, withdrew to her bedroom to ache in solitude because she had no children.

CHAPTER XVI.

In which Rose has to Restrain her Sympathies.

ROSE left the torn brocade. Her own worn heart needed stitches—many of them. She sat down, dumbly eloquent, on the hearthrug and thought how pleasant it would be to have a holiday from care. She prayed timidly for Edward. She tried to forget her knowledge of the world and the average ambitious girl. Would Chloe be the Exception? She remembered her eyes and felt hopeful.

Sir Harry Blythe was announced. For an awkward moment neither of them could speak. Then he expressed his pleasure at finding her in good health. She looked younger than her years and prettier than her features. Her auburn hair caught the sun and curled deliciously round her ears. He always noticed ears and insteps. Rose's ears were incredibly perfect. He peered nervously at her feet. They were as well formed as his own. He could face with confidence the thought of future generations. . . . They spoke of Mrs. Harrowby, her bitter charges against life.

"She over-estimates the power of money," said Sir Harry; "she thinks of nothing else. It has been her curse. Her tone is deplorable. And the joke is that both Chale and Harrowby had ample means! I believe they were both genuinely in love with her. But she was always longing to play Beggar-Maid to a King Cophetua. Only a brilliant woman could be so silly. . . . No doubt you think us a strange family. Take me, for example. I am selfish, worldly, cynical and indolent."

" I hope not," said Rose.

" I have, at any rate, always been told so," he rejoined, showing a bruised smile. " I know my reputation. We all know, as a matter of fact, what people think of us. But if I am, as I said before, selfish, I am by no means self-satisfied. A man's moral force depends almost wholly on his wife—or his women friends—but most of all on his wife. In my particular circle marriages have often to be made for more impersonal considerations than those of mere affection! If wives so married, however, would take the same trouble to attract and influence their husbands as they do to please their . . . admirers . . . many lives would be redeemed. I am by no means convinced that a man is naturally unfaithful. All the men I know are very anxious to do the right thing. They hate dishonor. When they go wrong it is always for . . . mainly . . . sentimental reasons. . . . I

see you wonder at my introducing this
subject. I will explain myself. My
aunt has not concealed from me that you
entertain a very strong feeling against
my . . . rumored . . . character. If you
did not condemn it—I should perhaps
esteem you less. I value a good woman's condemnation. But if you could
not excuse it—I should not be talking to
you now. The saints are always tolerant
of weaknesses in others; they alone
know how hard it is to be strong!"

The best of women—and the worst—
is never in such spiritual danger as when
some man would lead her to understand
that he regards her as a saint. The
temptation to at once prove and disprove
the charge is great. The difficulty of
sustaining the reputation—yet greater.
For, to be really saint-like, one has to be
pugnacious, and pugnacity is not charming. To say the true word in season and
out of season is a harsh, ungrateful task.

All thanks for the like are usually sobbed
over gravestones, old letters, and dusty
keepsakes. A loving woman deserves
much credit when she can cheerfully ab-
dicate all the heart's desire for tenderness
in favor of her coffin-lid. Rose had received many cold looks and bitter reproaches in her struggle to work good
rather than evil. Robsart's farewell note
made tearful reading. Edward's last
glance had fallen like hot cinders on her
face. And then the self-distrust which
followed all her efforts! Had she been
wise, after all, to leave Ottley? She
thought of Robsart's possible life in India. Mrs. Harrowby drew lurid pictures
of military society abroad. Edward's
sudden attachment to Chloe Crecy—how
would it end? Rose spent her anxious
nights dreaming prayers and crying in
her sleep. Philosophy could only give
her the fortitude to bear her own troubles.
When those she loved were suffering, or

in peril, her philosophy failed. In this respect she differed from many of the virtuous, who, in learning patience, forget compassion. . . .

"My career so far," continued Sir Harry, "has been a disappointment to my family. They feel that I have not made the best of my talents. I was considered a clever boy. It would be false modesty to deny this. I was probably bright. When I left Cambridge I went abroad. Art appealed to me. Politics were a bore. So I studied Art . . . from the outside, as it were. I never drew a line. I merely sought the principle of beauty in all things. What is beautiful is right: what is unbeautiful is wrong. You know the idea? But to *know* true beauty. That is a life-work."

Rose was listening intently. As he looked down at her he felt that there was not a wise man, aware of her infinite ability for self-sacrifice, her religious

method of idolatry, but would have
made every effort to secure the treasure
even at the cost of her own happiness.

"My circumstances were such," he
continued, "that, fortunately or unfor-
tunately, I could gratify every rational
caprice. I made mistakes. I admired
the wrong things. Perhaps the wrong
people. But I was never coarse. There
is sentiment in our family. My mother
was an amateur poetess of no inconsider-
able merit. She never published her
verses. She corresponded with Words-
worth; she knew Shelley. You may
imagine her."

Rose bowed her head.

"My earliest associations," said Sir
Harry, "were with all that is high-minded.
I abhor the base, the sordid, the igno-
minious. I observe human conduct, but
I do not presume to understand it. My
sole endeavor is to keep my own mind
varnished. I used that word deliberately.

I would not have you suspect me of self-deception. Life as a thing is hideous. Imagination is its sole redemption. It is our imagination, not our conscience, which makes us better than the beasts of the field. Conscience of itself makes us, if anything, the beast's inferior. For he represents nature warring honestly with natural forces. But we represent nature at war with God. . . ."

The man was sincere, or had—in the course of conversation—gradually become so. How long his sincerity would last was another—and perhaps an ungenerous—question. Few prayers would be answered—and fewer good intentions placed to our credit—if the Judge of all hearts demanded that same unswerving constancy of mind from us which we so urgently insist on from our fellow-creatures. To be wilfully honest with another human being for even half an hour is enough to establish some claim, at all

events, to an immortal soul. And it is
enough to explain the Divine desire to
save the same. A famous priest once
wrote, that the majority of sinners were
so excessively unpleasant that one wondered how the Almighty could feel love
for them. The answer seems plain.
With Him we are always in earnest,
and earnestness is irresistibly endearing.
Rose was too sympathetic to feel any
unkind amusement at what was purely
comic in Sir Harry's egoism. If it were
not for the egoists we should learn very
little about ourselves. That much is
clear. Blythe's sketch of his mother,
that amateur poetess, was not without
pathos—the inevitable laugh once done
with. Poetry—and most of all amateur
poetry—stands for pain. Every line of
it spells woe. Either the writer—or
those living with the writer—could tell a
tale. Sir Harry's face was engraved with
worn-out rhymes. *Heart* and *part, take*

and *forsake*, *love* and *above*, *dear* and *tear*, *to-day* and *away*, *kindness* and *blindness.* . . . But the man was now sincere. Was he ever—at his worst—*in*sincere? Rose could not think so. He had Manners, but he was never a sham.

"I wished to give you," he continued, "some faint notion of the life I had led. That is why I have dwelt at such unpardonable length on my point of view. No woman needs to understand more of any man's history than his point of view. That is the only thing she can affect— that she is competent—or called upon— to deal with. When I assure you that you have—quite unconsciously, I know —affected my whole mental attitude—I mean it as the highest compliment I can offer. Not that you value compliments."

"Oh dear!" said Rose, getting red and feeling wretched.

Sir Harry knew women. He did not misunderstand her blush. If a handsome

man can ever lose hope in a love-affair,
Blythe lost it then.

"I have been able to watch you more
closely than you can realize," he went
on, but in a duller voice. "Your patience, your dignity, your courage, your
tenderness. And I know your story.
I was acquainted, too, with your husband.
Your sorrow where your marriage is concerned was, and must always be, unspeak-
able. If I refer to it, it is merely to
show you that I understand."

He looked up and met her eyes. A
silent question was put; a silent answer
given.

"All the rest," he said, aloud, "shall not
now be put into words. I see that you,
too, understand. . . . I would have tried
to make you happy, Rose."

She was weeping, and he received an
exquisite satisfaction from her grief.
Each one of her tears fell like fiery rain
on his chilled heart. It evidently pained

her to refuse him. This is a woman's innocent snare for calling back, insidiously, rejected love.

"I should own," he said, "that my aunt has more than once hinted that your . . . interest . . . was elsewhere! I am too late!"

"My friend," she said, quickly, "now let *me* talk!"

Mother-like she patted his arm.

"I thank you," said she. "I wonder at you. You are rich, handsome, young, and popular. If you married me, all your relatives—with one exception—would call you a fool. Not that I should disgrace them or you. If I could call back my youth—my prettiness (and I was pretty once)—if I had a fortune, it would all be thought reasonable enough. But these things are not and cannot be. For some years now I have worked for my living. I am at present Mrs. Harrowby's companion."

"You would give me a future," said
Sir Harry, who had well and often
weighed all these objections; "you are
the one woman who has been able to
make me contemplate marriage not only
as a possible, but a desirable, state. You
are my ideal wife. I had no ideal till I
met you."

He was still sincere.

"That other man," he added, with
some bitterness, "is lucky. Does he
know—how lucky?"

"You are quite mistaken," said Rose,
trembling. "The . . . man . . . you refer to is my brother's friend. Circumstances threw us much—perhaps too
much—into each other's society. His
life was, I think, sadder than my own.
For he was a man. Men were made to
reform existence, not to accept it. Endurance on their part works like rust.
. . . I was sorry for him."

"And can't you feel sorry for *me*?"

cried Sir Harry, dropping the even tone and frigid air he mistook for self-control; " can't you feel sorry for *me?* You are my one chance. I know it. I love you."

He knelt at her feet. He put his arm round her waist.

" I know it," he repeated.

Rose unlocked his hand and moved away to the window.

"What can I say?" she asked.

He stood up, and, turning his back to her, watched her reflection in the mirror.

" Perhaps I spoke too eagerly," he observed, after a long pause. " I intended to be calm, but when I saw you looking so distressed about that—fellow—I said anything! You don't understand me. I am not made of stone. Let us talk quietly."

" Not on this subject," said Rose.

" I don't wish to persuade you into any step against your will. No happiness ever comes by persuasion. Nor will I

urge the fact that you ought to be married—and married to a man who can offer
you the means, the position you deserve.
Such considerations do not weigh with
you. My aunt tells me that when you
were a mere school-girl you refused
Charlie Aberthaw. He would have made
a better husband than Arden, and he
owns half of Mertford! You were foolish to reject him. Not that I wish to
remind you of old mistakes."

" You may," said Rose, serenely, " you
may. They give me courage."

" You are a strange woman. . . . Did
you wish me to believe that you find life
here—with my aunt—preferable to a life
of affection, tenderness . . . devotion .
. . independence ? It is inconceivable ! "

" If I married you," said Rose, " whose
heart would break ? "

Involuntarily, his hand pressed a letter-
case in his breast-pocket,

" What do you mean ? " he asked.

"Would any heart be broken?" she explained.

"No one," he answered, "would have any right to—to—say the least word."

"Not even Lady Lamister?"

"That's a preposterous rumor. . . . "

"I have often seen Lady Lamister," said Rose; "her face . . . her pitiful face —has told me all I know."

"She is not a happy woman.   I cannot help her expression!"

"You could!"

"You are wrong to introduce her name. I must call it—pardon me—unchivalrous. Another woman!   This is not like you."

"I never believe in a reform which looks, in the back, like desertion!" said Rose, ignoring his remark.

"Desertion," said Sir Harry, "is a most uncalled-for word."

"If Lady Lamister were an evil wo-man," continued Rose, "it would be different.   Your will is stronger than

hers—that is all. And, as you used your
will to her misfortune, now—that your
point of view is altered—use it for her
salvation. But to forsake her—because
—for a moment—another woman is in
sight! Is that being a changed man? It
sounds very like the old one!"

"You will certainly regret this . . .
this tone," replied Sir Harry. "There
are some things which ought never to be
said! They jar horribly. They haunt
the mind. They kill affection."

"I speak as your best friend," said Rose.

He laughed.

"I don't ask for your friendship," said
he. "Your friendship is too disinterested! I want love. If you loved me
you would not worry long about Lady
Lamister's broken heart!"

She made no answer.

"I shall go abroad," he said, abruptly.

"Why don't you marry Lady Lamister?"

He seemed not to hear.

"Good-bye," said he; "whether I agree with you—or whether I think you are unreasonable—I find myself your slave."

He had recovered his gallantry.

"I want you to do the right thing and be happy," said Rose.

His eyes were more desperate for a last look at her face than his ears to hear her advice. Yet her advice—as its echo reached him—seemed good. Hilda Lamister—with all her faults—was very sweet. She depended on him for her moral principles. Perhaps this was as it should be—if one wanted peace of mind. The reformation scheme had a seamy side. Poor little Hilda! She made scenes; she had lately taken to rouge; she went uneasily from church to church seeking "eloquent" preachers. Poor little Hilda, indeed!

"Pray for your own happiness, Rose," he said, solemnly; "not mine! not mine!"

And so he left her.

CHAPTER XVII.

Some Ways of Bearing Affliction.

ROSE carried Robsart's farewell letter
in her breast. She seldom re-read the
whole; her memory had adorned itself
with a few love-trimmed phrases picked
out here and there from the dim, gram-
matical gloom.

" I have enlisted because I am not rich enough
to travel as a civilian, and every association here is
now so painful that my sole cure lies in flight.
For the present, I am ill in mind—so ill that I
have neither the time nor the power to take my
choice of remedies. I accept—and accept grate-
fully—the first which offers itself. My soul is
drenched with bitterness. This, I know, from
your own example, is not right. I have never
heard you complain. So I must try to learn the
secret of endurance."

He did not ask her to write, and, woman-like, she felt at once relieved and hurt at this mark of consideration. A correspondence between people who may not, with mutual peace of mind, remain together under the same roof is the very sledge-hammer of woe. It shatters our rock of refuge about our ears. It crushes down every philosophic resolution. It is an unearthing of the buried—a tearing-up of the heart's sleeping grain. What is the secret of endurance but the willingness to concede that certain things can never be? Rose had said this often. She knew that Robsart had been thinking—when he wrote—of her own words. But circumstances were changed now. The impossible had become merely difficult. She sat musing, with her face buried in her hands and tears trickling through her fingers.

"Our Father," she prayed, "if there be any happiness laid up for me, let it be given rather to Edward."

She was roused by a tap on the shoulder. It was Mrs. Harrowby, grown very old and very small.

"I am afraid," said she, "that I spoke rather harshly to that poor boy."

Her voice quavered. She sat down; closed her eyes.

"Rose," she whispered, at last, "it's no use . . ." and she fell so violently to weeping that her face looked like a little white grave-stone in a great storm of rain.

"You understand!" she said, when she grew calmer.

Rose nodded her head.

"I have been thinking about your father," murmured Mrs. Harrowby. "I have never said bitter things about him, have I? His eyes were gray like pebbles, and his under-lip looked selfish. The last time we met, he asked me to let him know—now and again—what I was doing! And he knew he had broken my

heart—*knew* it, Rose. I was never coy
with Banish; I loved him far too seriously to play monkey-tricks. . . . But
that's all over. . . . I have a little cottage
in Mertford," she added, after a pause,
"which isn't grand enough for Harry
Blythe, though it's pretty and conven-
ient, and, for a man with a thousand a
year, it would be perfect. I will give
it to Edward and make him a suitable
allowance. The boy is a genius. You
must go to Ottley and tell him so to-
morrow. He shall have his chance.
There is something in him. Some people back horses: I prefer to back souls!"

She chattered on at a feverish pace.
The boy stood on the threshold of a
great artistic career; he craved encouragement. Every one would believe in
the successful; every one was ready to
help those who stood in no need of assistance, but beginners had a hard time.

" He has enough to live on, dear Mrs.

Harrowby," said Rose, "and if you are determined to be generous, it would be kinder to give his opera a hearing than to give him more money than he could wisely spend."

"You forget the girl. I want him to marry that girl. He loves her. She inspires him."

"She would cease to inspire him when he realized that someone else was paying their bills. He has a proud nature."

"He is a man of genius," said Mrs. Harrowby, "he will, in time, make a small fortune. He will not rest long on my feeble oars. I merely lend them while his own are being shaped. My bankers shall place to his credit one thousand a year, till he, himself, can earn as much. That's a fair proposal, and no reasonable person—in his circumstances —would refuse it."

She had telegraphed for her lawyer; the man arrived while she was talking.

Rose felt far from satisfied at her friend's course, and when, on the morrow, she left London for Ottley, her mind was beset with many doubts.

How strangely familiar Ottley looked on that day of returning! Adam was at the station with Arabella and the trap; the stationmaster and the porter and the boy at the paper stand were smiling on the platform; yet it was all changed, all different. Adam, ever a silent man, had little to say as they drove to the farm.

"My brother—Mr. Tatley—has lost his wife," he observed, but no more.

Adam's brother was always called *Mr.* Tatley, because he had once been valet to the Marquis of Garrow and he now betted. His wife was the village dressmaker.

"Poor soul! poor patient soul!" said Rose, "what will become of all of the little ones? Let us call at the cottage on the way home."

They found the widower sitting in an old smoking-jacket rocking his youngest born to sleep and reading *The Matrimonial Herald.*

"Pray do not rise," said Rose, "you will disturb the child. I am very sorry to hear——"

"Oh, madam," said Mr. Tatley, "it comes very hard. I have nine children. And there's no one to look after them. Susan has taken the five eldest for the time being, but that can't go on for ever."

"That's true," said Adam.

"Ethel was used to hard work, and she didn't feel it," continued Mr. Tatley; "it was nothing to her to get up at five and go on all day till ten or eleven. But I have never done that sort of thing. So a man is driven to be thoughtful," added he "in spite of himself."

"True," said Adam.

"But no Second," observed Mr. Tatley, "could ever be the same as the First!"

"And when was she buried?" asked Rose.

"Last week, madam," said Mr. Tatley; "and it was all done in good taste There was nothing vulgar, and we drank sherry afterwards."

Rose shook his hand and left one of her few sovereigns on the mantelpiece. Then she and Adam drove on to Wrestle's Farm.

"Mr. Tatley," remarked Adam, "is such a gentleman in his way of bearing trouble, that you would think he was a love-child!"

CHAPTER XVIII.

In which a Few are Found Faithful.

EDWARD was absent at the choir practice when Rose reached the farm, but
Susan stood in the doorway, her lips
heavy with undelivered news.

" Upon my heart and life," said she, " I
have been all of a tremble since I got
your telegram. I have shaken every car-
pet in the house—such a to-do I never
made, not even when I was married.
You do look a poor mite, and no mistake!
Have some milk, there's a lamb! And
what goings-on since you were here!
What with Mr. Edward and poor Maude-
Ethel Tatley's death!—But come up-
stairs to your room, darling, and see the
lovely water-can I bought you when I

went into Ottley Major for the funeral.
I see it hanging up in Bolton s window—
the very thing. Let me untie your bonnet— 'twould suit you better, dearie, if
you curled your hair. But it don't look
well, say what you like, to see a lot of
curls on a recent widow! Oh, my dear,
when I heard *that !* Well, there !—it
didn't seem quite right to say, 'Thank
God,' so I went to church three times the
Sunday after and followed the Prayer-
book most particular. I sang the Psalms
so loud that Mrs. Triptree looked round
as if I was drowning the choir. *'To him
which slew great kings : for His mercy endureth for ever.'* You should ha' heard
me shout that. *'And Og, the king of
Bashan : for His mercy endureth for ever.'*
The Bible is a grand blessing when you
can't trust yourself to speak natural.
When I said ' Og,' I thought of Mr. Arden and——"

"Tell me, dear Susan," said Rose, kiss-

ing her apple-ish cheeks, "tell me all you
can about Edward. Is he well? does he
eat his porridge?"

"There's too much herb-mooning in
this neighborhood," replied Susan, with
a wise look; "but from all I can hear it
is much the same everywhere! Mr.
Edward has given up porridge, and he
lives on Normandy pippins, sardines,
anchovy paste, and olives in bottles. His
stomach seems to turn against sensible
food. It does sometimes—when you fall
in love. At the time father was courting
mother, she couldn't touch nothing but
raw turnips. She used to tell that story
by the hour. Love is a cruel thing for
the indigestion. And I have heard that
Miss Chloe Crecy ain't much better off.
She's taking orange wine and iron four
times a day. She's got a heart—poor
dear young lady—in spite of herself.
She'll have Mr. Edward yet. They say
that the way she keeps the Honorable

Camelot so near and yet so far is a lesson
to menials.   He dursn't ask her to marry
him, and yet he dursn't go away for fear
of Mr. Edward.   Mrs. Crecy is on the
rampage, and Mr. Crecy goes on something dreadful in his dressing-room of a
morning and evening.   He shouts through
the door to Mrs. Crecy while she's doing
her hair, and the second housemaid, who
sweeps the landing outside, told me that
he talks so blasphemiously that she has
scruples in listening!   But, as she says,
the landing must be swept, and before
breakfast, too!   I don't feel a bit of
worry about Mr. Edward, my pet, not a
bit.   He's such a lovely-looking feller
without his beard.   How that did spoil
him, to be sure!   You mark my words—
he'll cut out the Honorable Camelot.   I
see Miss Crecy heave her eye up to the
organ-loft more than once during the
Communion last Sunday, when every one
was praying with their heads down!   Of

course, it wasn't right to be looking at a
young man just then, but flesh-and-blood
will wander, even if you was to glue your
knees to a hassock! No, lovie, the only
minit that I felt downright bad since you
left was when Mr. Robsart went away
with the Sergeant. I couldn't watch him
go. I stayed in the back pantry, and I
kep' saying to myself, 'Whatever will
become of poor darlin' Mrs. Arden?'
You see, dearie, I *knew*."

"What?" said Rose, with a fine blush.

"I knew, dearie," said Susan, solemnly,
"that you loved him to your life! I
knew it all along—but you don't mind
me, surely. It used to go to my heart
when you would sit at work a-trying to
act more Christian than is good for the
skin. And it was a crool test for any
man—say what you like—to see a sweet,
pretty young creature growing downright
plain, just out of duty, so to speak. You
are always nice-looking to me, darlin',

but I have often wished that you could
ha' worn your lovely hair in ringlets and
shown off.   As for Mr. Robsart, he
couldn't deceive Susan.   I have caught
him—more'n once—picking up your
work—after you had left it—and giving
it a look in an adoring sort of way as he
knew would ha' been wrong to give to
you direct!   And once he kissed it—and
a needle pricked him—which narrer-
minded people would have called a judgment, but I think it was a accident and
nothing more.   I was never one for finding judgments!   If a man was to kiss his
own wife's sewing-basket (to be sure, I
never see'd one do anything so affection-
ate), he'd be certain to get a darning-
needle in his chin.   There's reason in all
things.   But now, my poor lamb, you can
think of him all day and all night without
sin (and after all you've gone through
you deserve a little happiness), and you
can put flowers on his mother's grave and

behave just as though you was engaged
to him! Won't it be heavenly, dear?
And he'll come back to England the very
moment he hears that you are free, and
sha'n't I cry at the wedding!"

The good creature had moist eyes at
this luxurious thought.

"And you can wear mauve or gray,"
she continued, after a pause, "or a nice
flowered silk—one of them that will stand
alone. They're a great support when
you feel your limbs giving way with pal-
pitations. And I've heard that one is
more nervous the second time o' getting
married than the first. Who could wonder
at it? But he'll make a kind husband—
will Mr. Robsart—although he's so quiet."

Rose kissed her again, and said "No!
no!" in an affirmatory tone.

"He won't come back for years and
years," said she; "and he doesn't even
know that things are different."

"Oh yes, he does," replied Susan, "for

I took and wrote to him myself. 'P. S.,' I says in my letter, 'I suppose you have heard our sad news. Mrs. Arden's husband has been mercifully took away after a heavy meal. Will send particulars in my next.' I thought that would do for a first hint."

"Oh, Susan!" said Rose, "how could you?"

"Because I knew you *wouldn't*," said Susan, stolidly.

Their conversation was interrupted at this point by a tap at the door.

"It's Georgiana," said Susan; "you wouldn't believe the trouble I have had with that girl. She mopes about the house and she ain't a bit the better for the nice outing I gave her to Maude-Ethel Tatley's funeral. But, oh, my dear!— that's an affair! Mr. Tatley has taken quite a fancy to her. Don't stand there knocking, Georgiana," she said, raising her voice, "but come in."

"Mr. Tatley is in the kitchen," said Georgiana, entering the room with a blush and a curtsey to Rose.

"What does *he* want now?" said Susan; but, as she spoke, her eyes fell upon a pair of jet earrings of the *drop*-shape which hung from Georgiana's scarlet ears.

"Who gave you them expensive presents?" she asked.

"Mr. Tatley," said Georgiana, simpering.

"That's the way it goes on!" exclaimed Susan; "of course, jet is mourning, and so far it's very delicate on Mr. Tatley's part. But it's early days, to my thinking, to be giving you even mourning jewelry! I don't hold with it myself, and I shall tell him so. They're a very handsome pair of earrings, those, such as any lady might wear. Maude-Ethel did speak once or twice of leaving them to me. She had 'em given to her while she

was in service at Squire Deane's. I
shall speak my mind to Tatley pretty
straight."

"And now, Georgiana," said Rose,
when Susan had flounced out of the
room, "have you forgotten Arthur?"

"La, ma'am," said Georgiana, "do you
mean Arthur Venus with the curly hair?
He went and 'listed. He never asked
me to remember him. And he's gone
clean out of my head. Young men are
so unsteady, too."

She felt her earrings, and looked pen-
sive.

"Poor Arthur!" said Rose.

"He wasn't kind to me," answered
Georgiana, getting white, "and no girl
with a bit o' pride could put up wi' such
treatment. And I demeaned myself being seen with him. They're a very common lot—the Venuses. Father would
ha' cast me off for marrying any one so
low. It's a lucky thing my eyes was

opened in time.   Now Mr. Tatley, as any
one can see, is a man in a thousand.   Mr.
Crecy offered to take him on as valet,
and so has Sir Robert Drame.   Mr. Crecy
offers the best wages, so he thinks he
'ull go there.   You don't see no company neither at Sir Robert's, and the
food 'ud poison a pauper. . . .   Besides,
Mr. Tatley likes to be near his fam'ly
and his friends ! "

She looked self-conscious, and glanced
at herself in the mirror on Rose's dressing-table.

"How did it all come about ? " asked
Rose, who was now resting, after her
long journey, on the sofa.

"It was like this," said Georgiana :
"Mrs. Tatley died, and the baby, too.
They was put in the same coffin.   I did
croi to see them there.   And it was all
through my croi-ing that Mr. Tatley
noticed me.   'You've got a feelin' heart,
Georgiana,' says he.   He was standin' by

the coffin at the time, shaking his head
and now and again holdin' up his ribs.
'I feel such a sinkin',' says he; 'I've got
the very same symtims as his lordship
had when her ladyship died o' typhoid at
Men*tone*. Just for all the world the very
same symtims. I remember they gave
his lordship a dose of brandy.' And
would you believe it, ma'am, not one of
the others who was there had the sense
to see what poor Mr. Tatley wanted.
He didn't like to ask right out for it—
he's not so vulgar. And I happened to
have the ten-shilling piece in my pocket
what you sent me for my birthday. I
was going to buy myself them amber
beads in Warton's window, but I slipped
round to 'The Plover and Quail' and
ordered in two bottles of the best
invalid brandy for Mr. Tatley. It's
something dreadful to see a man so
upset."

"And then what happened?" asked
Rose.

"He shook my hand, and he said I
was the sort as would make a home
happy. And I says, 'Not I'; and he
says, 'If the funeral wasn't on my mind, I
could stand here talking to you all day';
and I says, 'Oh, Mr. Tatley! I'm sure
I'm nothing to look at'; and he says,
'What's looks in the mother of a family?'
And I says, half-laughin', 'I'm not the
mother of a family.' 'No,' says he, 'but
I know a family as you could be a mother
to.' And then his eldest—who is just
turned eleven and is bandy—came in and
we didn't say no more."

"Poor Arthur!" said Rose.

Georgiana's under-lip began to twitch
and she smoothed her apron—as though
that movement could calm the agitation
of her mind.

"I don't wish to think about him,
ma'am," she answered; "it's quite bad

enough to wake up in the morning and to feel a holler feeling in your side, as if your heart had been hacked out. I used to be very fond o' thinking, once, but now, when I am alone, I says over hymns to myself—' A few more years shall roll,' and ' O Paradise! O Paradise!' Then if Susan finds me croi-ing, she knows it's the sad words I'm croi-ing over and no young man."

She turned away as she spoke, and looked out of the window.

"There's Mr. Edward, ma'am," she said, and, with averted face, left the room.

Rose murmured a little prayer that all might be well with her brother, and hastened down the stairs to meet him. His countenance was radiant, and he embraced her with all the boisterous affection of his school days.

"Three cheers!" he cried, and fairly lifted her off her feet. She was a small

woman, and was not much heavier than a
girl of fourteen.

"Three cheers!" he cried again. He
pulled her into the sitting-room, where
he threw himself far back on the hard
sofa, crossed his legs, and put his arms
behind his head.

"She has promised to wait," he said;
"Chloe has promised to wait. She refused that ass Camelot last night."

Each member of the small household
at Wrestle's Farm had a word to offer
on the subject of Miss Chloe Crecy's
sudden decision. Susan maintained that
"looks had won the day." Georgiana
sighed, and said "any girl could be true
if she had a comfortable home and no
living to get." Adam was disposed to
think that the heiress had been won over
by "gab"—a power which he himself
had certainly found irresistible when
Susan used to court him at the hay-mak-
ing. Rose, who said nothing, took, se-

cretly, the greater part of Edward's happiness as a miraculous answer to her own prayers—and who shall say that she was mistaken? It was because she had seen so many prayers fulfilled that she feared to make frequent petitions. But while she saw the accomplishment of her entreaty, she did not forget its terms. She had chosen Edward's welfare before her own, and God seems never to reject a self-sacrifice. He accepts what is offered Him, and requires it often with usury. Rose knew this as she smiled on Edward's eager bliss. She delivered Mrs. Harrowby's message, but even while she told it, a telegram from London summoned her to Cavendish Square.

"Perhaps she has changed her mind," said Edward.

Rose shook her head and did not name her fear. She remembered that last faint look on Mrs. Harrowby's face. Though she left Ottley by the mail the same

night, she reached London next day too
late. The blinds of the house were all
down—excluding the sunlight—for Mrs.
Harrowby had not been called that
morning and still slept.

CHAPTER XIX.

The Last.

MRS. HARROWBY had altered her will on the night before her death, and she left three-fourths of her large fortune to be divided equally between Rose Arden and Edward Banish, the children of her dearly-loved friend, the late Edward Banish, Esq., Q.C. The remaining fourth was bequeathed to Sir Harry Blythe. This testament was, of course, contested by several relatives, and great sums of money were spent in proving that Rose was neither an adventuress nor a witch. The case might have dragged on for many months and become a *cause célèbre*, but for the frightful distraction which suddenly presented itself to the public

mind in the shape of the Indian Mutiny.
Robsart was indeed doomed to learn the
secret of endurance. Rose's suffering
during that terrible period may not be
told. She became housekeeper to Edward and Chloe, and spent her new
income mainly on her sister-in-law's
pleasures. The marriage was, in many
senses, fortunate, and as for Edward's
success—is it not known? Have we not
heard his light operas and his tragic
songs? Have we not said that but for
his prosperity he might have been our
English Mozart? Rose, however, had
paid such a price for his happiness, that,
being a true woman, she became a Philis-
tine in her judgment of his art. So long
as he was well and contented, she thought
it absurd to worry about the weak or-
chestration of a *Symphony in D.* Her
pretty auburn hair turned gray, and when
she attended a dinner party given in
honor of Sir Harry Blythe and his bride

(the widow of Lord Lamister), her ladyship made a loud comment in the drawing-
room to the effect that "Mrs. Arden was
the woman who had set her cap at poor
Harry. As if she could have had the
least chance, etc., etc. And her tricks
were so transparent."

Even of such thickness are this world's
transparencies!

Two anxious years passed by before
Robsart returned to England. He had
won wounds, experience, and the Victoria
Cross; but he found poor Rose's fingers
too thin for the Indian rings he had
brought with him to place upon them.
When the sorely-tried soul wept her joy
on his breast, she sobbed a question about
Arthur Venus. (Georgiana had married
Mr. Tatley and become a shrew.) ·

"Arthur Venus," said Robsart, "has
a wooden leg and half his head shaved
off. And I suppose you wish, for his

mother's sake, that *I* had the wooden leg instead !"

Most of us are aware that when Colonel Robsart, V. C., retired from the army, he represented Ottley in the House of Commons. And perhaps some of us have met his wife, and wondered why he did not choose a brilliant-looking woman with a Presence. For if you have prayed many years under the Herb-Moon, your figure does not look stylish to the vulgar. But Robsart, who, it is said, will be in the next Cabinet, and is moreover a very handsome man, seems to carry marital devotion to the point of idolatry—a mistake which those distinguished beauties, Lady Shawcrosse and the Duchess of Man, find inexcusable.

But you and I, my reader, may understand him better.

www.ingramcontent.com/pod-product-compliance
Lightning Source LLC
Chambersburg PA
CBHW020604260626
47157CB00003B/864